REVELATION

— OF —

ROYALTY

BILL WINSTON

REVELATION
— OF —
ROYALTY

CHARISMA
HOUSE

Visit the author's website at www.billwinston.org.

Library of Congress Cataloging-in-Publication Data:
An application to register this book for cataloging has been submitted to the Library of Congress.
International Standard Book Number: 978-1-63641-009-8
E-book ISBN: 978-1-63641-010-4

While the author has made every effort to provide accurate internet addresses at the time of publication, neither the publisher nor the author assumes any responsibility for errors or for changes that occur after publication. Further, the publisher does not have any control over and does not assume any responsibility for author or third-party websites or their content.

21 22 23 24 25 — 9 8 7 6 5 4 3 2 1
Printed in the United States of America

CONTENTS

PREFACE

I HAVE BEEN LED to write many books, but this one that you are holding is perhaps one of the most important given the times we are living in. Today, we as believers must know and walk in the revelation of our royalty in Christ.

Those who are familiar with my teachings know that I have preached and taught faith in God's Word for decades. I know from personal witness that without faith it is impossible to please God, to get things done in the earth, or to reach our God-given destiny while here on earth.

However, I have also learned that while many believers think they have a faith problem (like the disciples did in Luke 17:5 when they cried out, "Lord, increase our faith"), what they really have is an image problem.

Even after their new birth in Jesus Christ, many Christians still have an image of inferiority and shortage that entered mankind when Adam and Eve fell in the Garden of Eden. When God put them out of the garden, mankind lost more than provision and fellowship with the Father. They also lost their royal identity.

The good news is that Jesus Christ restored this royal identity to everyone who would believe in His name. The revelation of this good news—the revelation of our royalty—is what I share on the pages of this book along with my life experiences that demonstrate this revelation.

Let me share one such experience. Without question, the greatest moment of my life was when I surrendered my life to the Lord Jesus Christ. I became born again, and instantly it felt like heavy weights had lifted off of me. But it wasn't too long after that joyous encounter that I fell into Satan's trap of still trying to pay for my sins.

At the time, I was living in a spacious three-bedroom apartment, driving a beautiful sports car, and enjoying a comfortable standard of living as a successful computer salesman. But guilt caused me to downsize my luxury apartment and sell my expensive sports car (at such a cheap price a man later told me, "You gave that car away!"), replacing it with an old, broken-down, rusted-out subcompact that barely ran. I downsized or ended good, long-standing friendships too.

I came into the kingdom of God with good self-esteem (even as an unbeliever). I had been a decorated fighter pilot and a successful businessman and had other life experiences that affirmed my dignity and value. But I slowly allowed the enemy to steal that esteem.

What was I doing when I gave everything away? I was trying to clear my conscience of guilt and shame for things I had done before I got saved. I was seeking to please God by living in poverty, thinking that made me humble.

According to Hebrews 11:6, the way I could have pleased God was to use my faith to pay off the note on my sports car, buy the entire apartment building (which was about to be made into condos), and convert my friends by demonstrating this new life in the kingdom. Unfortunately, a sense of unworthiness will not let you think like this. Sin-consciousness won't allow you to receive *big* from God, and Satan knows it takes *a revelation* (not information) to get beyond this barrier. Thus, I have written this book, *Revelation of Royalty.*

Revelation 19:16 says, "And he hath on his vesture and on his thigh a name written, KING OF KINGS, AND LORD OF LORDS." God calls us kings.

Here are some things to know about a king (and this title includes women):

- A king can do no wrong. By referring to that well-known maxim, I'm not saying kings don't make mistakes. I mean they aren't oppressed by the sin-consciousness I spoke of previously. They are free from shame because they realize they are new creatures in Christ (2 Cor. 5:17) and righteous through Him (2 Cor. 5:21). "The king speaks with divine authority; his decisions are always right" (Prov. 16:10, GNT).

- A king lives by decree. A king doesn't ask for anything. He declares what he wants, and those in his world rush to see that it is done. "Where the word of a king is, there is power" (Eccles. 8:4).

- A king has no fear. A lion is considered the fearless king of the jungle. Proverbs says the lion is the "strongest among beasts, and turneth not away for any" (30:30). He is fearless. We believers are descendants of the Lion of the tribe of Judah, the King of kings and Lord of lords.

The Holy Spirit is inside of us to tutor us into greatness. He knows that as it was with Mephibosheth in 2 Samuel chapter 9, condemned people cannot receive their inheritance even though they are in a royal family. Only those who know who they are can receive the things that rightfully belong to them. In fact, your inheritance comes in proportion to your new identity.

This is why I wrote this book—to help you see yourself as God sees you and get a revelation of your royalty.

Enjoy!

PART I

TAKE YOUR PLACE

——⟶ IN THE ⟵——

KINGDOM

CHAPTER 1

YOUR ROYAL IDENTITY

✦————————✦

LET ME REMIND you who you are.

You are a member of the royal family of God, the Sovereign over all the universe. You are pictured in His most treasured family portraits. You are a child of the King of all kings, the supreme ruler over heaven and earth. He loves you and has given you great authority and powerful assignments as a member of His eminent ruling family.

You possess royal privileges, royal perspective, royal demeanor, and royal wealth. You are protected and empowered in every particular way, and you exercise supernatural authority over the earth, just as your Father does. His strength is available to you in every form, in every manner, and in every situation. You are designed to rule, reign, and decree His will in this realm and in the realm of angels and principalities.

You are free from the curse, released from all toil, unburdened to soar, prepared to prosper, fashioned to rule, equipped to lead. All of this flows from your royal identity, which can never be changed. It is who you are forever.

FROM THE BEGINNING

There are some who might call this nothing more than happy talk and empty encouragement. But it is actual fact. Let me assure you that the Bible speaks—shouts, really—that you are royalty, from the first chapter to the last. Your princely position is not human invention or clever construction—it is God's unchangeable idea. The great need in the body of Christ today is to discover, or rediscover, who we are and act once again like royalty on the earth.

Let me trace your royal lineage. Did you know that your family line goes back to Genesis 1? Nobody has a greater claim on being a son or daughter of Adam and Eve than you do, because all humans descend from this original pair. You were literally born into a royal line. Humanity's first home, a place called Eden, was nothing less than an outpost of heaven on the earth—an extension of heaven that was never meant to be cut off through sin.

In Eden, God modeled His plans for your family and mine, the human race. He taught Adam to steward heavenly realities, heavenly kingdoms, heavenly wealth. To His first children God conferred the same power and ability He used to create this earth. This is a monumental statement. As children of the King, they were given power to continue the work of God and make every place on the earth just like the Garden of Eden. Here is how the Bible summarizes God's assignment to our ancestors.

> And God blessed them, and God said unto them, Be
> fruitful, and multiply, and replenish the earth, and
> subdue it: and have dominion over the fish of the
> sea, and over the fowl of the air, and over every
> living thing that moveth upon the earth.
>
> —GENESIS 1:28

Adam and Eve's job was to cause heavenly reality
to spread across the rest of the planet. Eden was their
training ground, their model, their initial home. God's
idea was that everything in the world outside the Garden
of Eden would come to look like Eden through human
beings' royal exercise of power. This remains the body of
Christ's assignment today. We were made to carry seeds
of heavenly realities into every place and situation we
encounter.

The kingdom of God inside of us—which expresses
itself through our values, morals, and creativity and in
many other ways—is by design greater than anything
else in the world. The fruit we bear is of a higher order—
a heavenly order. This is why God's royal children grow
and become greater than those around us wherever we
are planted. This is the nature of the kingdom: to thor-
oughly influence and saturate every environment on
earth.

It is our responsibility and joy to walk in these
assignments!

FALLING TO THE CURSE LEVEL

Of course, we know how things went. Adam, through disobedience, caused humanity to fall to the level of the curse. Genesis chapter 2 says:

> And the LORD God took the man, and put him into the garden of Eden to dress it and to keep it. And the LORD God commanded the man, saying, Of every tree of the garden thou mayest freely eat: but of the tree of the knowledge of good and evil, thou shalt not eat of it: for in the day that thou eatest thereof thou shalt surely die.
> —GENESIS 2:15–17

All humanity was in Adam, which is why the Bible says "all have sinned, and come short of the glory of God" (Rom. 3:23) and "the wages of sin is death" (Rom. 6:23). More than something we did, sin is how we were born. Having all been born in sin, we all must be born again. This reunites us with our royal prerogatives and assignments on the earth.

But while the curse came, our identity in God's eyes didn't change—not one bit. No curse is powerful enough to change God's ultimate plan.

- He created a race of children (a new species) to be like Him in identity and power. He gave us the assignment of bringing heaven to earth.

- His will for us does not waver over time! He is the same yesterday, today, and forever.

- God's plans are so good that He never has to change His mind. His purpose for His children has been fixed since Genesis 1 and remains fixed today—in your life and mine.

In fact, just to be sure we understood our founding purpose, God repeated the same mandate He had given to Adam numerous times throughout the Bible. For example, God spoke to Noah the same blessing He spoke to Adam and Eve:

> And God blessed Noah and his sons, and said unto them, Be fruitful, and multiply, and replenish the earth.
>
> —GENESIS 9:1

In Genesis 12, God selected Abram (later called Abraham) to walk in this same royal identity. By doing so, Abraham became your grandfather. God promised him, "I will make of thee a great nation, and I will bless thee, and make thy name great; and thou shalt be a blessing: and I will bless them that bless thee, and curse him that curseth thee: and in thee shall all families of the earth be blessed" (vv. 2–3).

This promise referred to you specifically. In the letter to the believers in Galatia, Paul made this clear, writing, "And if ye be Christ's, then are ye Abraham's seed, and heirs according to the promise" (Gal. 3:29).

I'm not giving you pixie dust and poetry—I'm spelling

out your literal family reality. If you are a believer in Christ, you are the seed and heir of Abraham. God's Word promises that you will be blessed the same way God blessed Abraham. You will have everything Abraham had, including great wealth and friendship with God. In fact, you will have these in greater measure than your father Abraham did because the kingdom of God is always expanding and increasing.

We have a greater revelation and relationship with God through His Son, Jesus Christ. In fact the Bible says that once we are born again, we become "joint-heirs with Christ" (Rom. 8:17). This means we have Jesus' own inheritance! Whatever He gets, we get. What will Jesus receive? Scripture says He was slain "to receive power and riches and wisdom, and strength and honor and glory and blessing" (Rev. 5:12, NKJV). Because we are coheirs with Christ, these blessings are available to every member of the body of Christ. We eternally possess the authority and means to change, rearrange, and subdue any place on earth to the glory of God.

You may be in a low place right now. You may have made many sinful mistakes and are in a bad condition in your life. Or you may have succeeded greatly but feel empty and disconnected from your ultimate purpose. The solution for every one of us is the same: reclaiming our royal identity. Your royal identity will turn mourning into joy, poverty into plenty, suffering into salvation, failure into success, and so much more. It will take you beyond all limitations that people—or maybe even you— have put on you. It does not matter how broken down or chaotic your life situation has become; your royal identity will solve any problem.

But you have to know who you are.

EMBRACING OUR ORIGINAL IMAGE

People have no choice but to be royal. God has "commanded the blessing." (See Deuteronomy 28:8.) He cannot and will not take it back—ever. The blessing of our royal nature cannot be overridden by people, principalities, or the devil himself. There isn't anything you have done that can stand in the way of your royal identity operating in your life. Period.

But while we cannot change our identity, we do have mastery over how much of our inheritance we walk in. Your inheritance, flowing down from Adam and Abraham, manifests in proportion to the self-image you embrace by faith. One man of God said it this way: "Your inheritance comes only in proportion to your new identity." Most of what we receive is based on our image. The question is, Do you see yourself with it? If you don't, you won't get it. You can blame people and powers and institutions and politicians and bosses and neighbors and so on, but as my hero Booker T. Washington liked to quote from Scripture, "As [a man] thinketh in his heart, so is he" (Prov. 23:7). What you believe is what you become. What you believe about yourself is where you end up.

Listen carefully to me: What you receive is not just about what you want; it's about what image you have of yourself. That image becomes the magnet attracting like unto like. It determines the amount of your inheritance that you will possess.

In 2 Corinthians 3:18, Paul says we are changing into the same image as Jesus. That seems like an amazing statement. Yet what did God say at the beginning? "Let us make man in our image" (Gen. 1:26). Paul's statement is amazing only when we sell ourselves short on who we are. The first thing God does when you are born again is fellowship with you. But you can't fellowship with somebody who is not on your level, so to speak. So He immediately goes to work on your self-image, assuring you that He made you like Him, in His image. You belong in His company.

It is almost blasphemous to degrade an image that God made to reflect His own. Your image cannot be compromised by your past or your problems. This image has no basis in color. It has no basis in background. Your image is perfect and timeless—you need only to joyfully declare and affirm that this is who you are.

INSIST ON YOUR IDENTITY

God has structured His kingdom so that everything is received by faith, so we must walk in our royalty by faith. The Bible says, "As he [Jesus] is, so are we in this world" (1 John 4:17). God sees you not in your present position but as the royalty He made you to be. You are literally one spirit with Jesus (1 Cor. 6:17) and made in His image!

- You have His life.

- You have His mind.

- You have His nature.

- You have His Spirit.

- You have His name.

- You have His ability.

- You have His disposition.

- You have His blessing.

- You have His faith.

- You have His love.

All these things and a million more are inside of you because you are God's image bearer. You can declare loudly (and I encourage you to do so!), "I am made in God's image and likeness. I have His Spirit. I have His mind. I have His love," and so on. Take ownership of your identity. Take ownership of your assignment. God has already designated your victory. He has already determined that you are invincible, indestructible, unstoppable, and indispensable. As He is, so are you in this world! "Now thanks be unto God, which always causeth us to triumph in Christ" (2 Cor. 2:14).

Abraham had to learn to see himself as the father of a great nation. Mary had to see herself as the one to give birth to the Messiah, the Son of God. Gideon had to see himself as a mighty man of valor. Nehemiah had to see himself as a wall builder. On and on it goes. For us to do the works of God, we first must grasp the image He has of us. We must believe that His mighty works can be done through us, and greater works than these will you do (John 14:12). As royal children of the Most High God, we have been empowered by our Creator to bring forth

the most powerful government the world has ever seen—
the kingdom of God.

Let's embrace our original image and walk in our
kingly and queenly assignments. This befits our royal
status and is the fruit of our royal nature. How do we
carry this out? Let's take a closer look.

CHAPTER 2

KINGS AND QUEENS IN GOD'S GOVERNMENT

RE YOU THE take-charge type? Are you the one who likes to set the agenda, occasionally boss a few people around, and get stuff done? Do you firmly believe your ideas should change the world? If so, that's just your royal nature coming out! You can't change it. It's how you were made—to rule and to reign.

Each of us was created by design with a dominion mindset. In Genesis 1, God said, "Let us make man in our image...and let them have dominion" (v. 26). Notice God didn't say, "Let us have dominion." He said, "Let them have dominion." *Them* was Adam and Eve. This is a huge statement, because as Adam's descendants, we have been given that dominion. It never went away. It is the inheritance of God's children.

This inheritance is God's rulership of the earthly realm, which He determined to share with us. We are His eternal partners in this plan. This is why Ephesians 5:1 says, "Therefore be imitators of God [copy Him and follow His example], as well-beloved children [imitate their father]" (AMPC). How do we follow His example? By establishing His government everywhere He sends us.

LITTLE CAESARS

Most people in Western countries don't understand the word *dominion*. In fact, it scares many of them. Westerners are accustomed to democracy, republics, and governments founded and controlled by the people and for the people. In other words, Westerners like being in charge of their governments. In democracies and democratic republics, the general population has power to make laws. In a fallen world system, these may be the best types of governments because they help to keep total power out of the hands of any one person. But our Western thinking does not accurately reflect the structure of the government of God.

God is perfect. He does not need to be limited or balanced out.

This is why God's government is not democratic; it's theocratic. It is sovereign. It is a monarchy, the rule of the King and His family. Many Westerners recoil at the thought of being led by kings, monarchs, and sovereigns because throughout history those leaders subjugated people, trampling their legal protections and rights. In American history, those who wielded the power abused it through slavery. But we have not lived under the perfect King and the dominion of His obedient children. That is God's chosen plan for the earth, and it marks every assignment, big or small, that He gives us in our individual lives.

Jesus Christ came ultimately to rule. When Western

Christians sum up Jesus' assignment, they typically say, "He preached the gospel, healed the sick, and gave His life to atone for our sins." This is all true, but consider His first words in ministry: "Repent: for the kingdom of heaven is at hand" (Matt. 4:17). His first command to all humanity was to repent for not having a kingdom mindset! There is no such thing as a kingdom without a king. Jesus did not come just to heal and preach but to reteach the kingdom. He had to change the way the people thought to get them to act the way they were made to behave. He had to reintroduce them to Garden of Eden realities—kingdom rule—to get the people to realize their royalty.

Again, Jesus' message was not, "Get saved so you too can escape this corrupt earth and go to heaven forever. We'll just leave the earth to sinners." No! His message was, "Heaven is coming to earth just as God always intended. The plan has not changed, and neither has your identity. You may have forgotten your identity, but now it's time to repent of that and embrace your dominion mindset again. You are My coheirs, My joint rulers, and it's time to step up!" His kingdom is a kingdom of kings—that's you and me! The Bible tells us we have "the mind of Christ" (1 Cor. 2:16), which is the dominion mindset of Jesus, who is coming back to rule and reign as "King of kings, and Lord of lords" (1 Tim. 6:15), the Sovereign over a royal, ruling family.

DOMINION, NOT DOMINATION

Dominion does not mean to selfishly dominate. Rather, it speaks of territory, jurisdiction, rule, management,

15

kingship, governance. We establish a royal standard everywhere we go by exercising godly stewardship and ownership. We take care of the earth for God. We serve others with the authority we are given. We were made to be in charge here. It was never meant for you and me to grope for things or to struggle for faith. God expected Adam and all those who came after him to function as fully empowered representatives of the royal household.

We see this model hiding in plain sight in the Gospels, where the Roman ruler, Caesar, placed people like Herod and Pilate over jurisdictions to rule as his representatives. These were ungodly men in a violent and idolatrous empire, but the governmental structure of that empire—and many other empires—was more like God's kingdom government than many modern, Western ones are. Rulers like Herod and Pilate did not represent themselves but Caesar. This is why they were afraid when Israel's religious leaders threatened them by saying, "If you don't do this, you are not Caesar's friend." (See John 19:12–15.) The last thing they wanted was to be reported to Caesar for not running their jurisdictions according to his will. If they did that, Caesar could recall them. So they functioned in their dominion mandate from Rome.

When the children of God function in their royal identity, it blesses the entire earth. No one is oppressed, disenfranchised, or disempowered as many were in Rome (and Babylon and every other godless government of man). In God's kingdom everything and everyone is elevated to a much higher standard in every area of life. But when God's children do not function in their royal identity, it spells disaster for all society. Ecclesiastes says,

"Woe to thee, O land, when thy king is a child...Blessed art thou, O land, when thy king is the son of nobles" (10:16–17).

Unless we behave as the royalty we are, there is a woe on the land. That is one big reason Jesus said there are serious consequences for blocking people from living in their dominion mandate. In Matthew 23:13, Jesus told powerful religious leaders, "Woe unto you...for ye shut up the kingdom of heaven against men: for ye neither go in yourselves, neither suffer ye them that are entering to go in." These religious leaders were literally keeping people from entering into the Genesis 1 dominion mandate for their lives. How dangerous! In a pathetic effort to control their followers, they deprived people of the royal image that would empower them to carry out kingdom assignments. This brought certain woe on the land.

We must reject the corrupt thinking of the world system, which tries to discredit the King and cancel the calling of every son and daughter of God. We must become unacculturated and de-traditionalized from our Western modes of thought, which invalidate the form and structure of God's government. We must study the one true kingdom to develop the kings and queens in us. "Repent: for the kingdom of heaven is at hand!"

THE PRODIGAL SON'S REVELATION OF ROYALTY

One of the clearest pictures in the Bible of a person realizing his royalty is the story Jesus told about a royal son who initially rejected his royal image. (See Luke 15:11–32.) This man is often called the prodigal son, but in truth he is a hero in the story—and in many ways his journey represents yours and mine.

The prodigal son was born into wealth, high position, and authority, just like we are. His father had much, but this son possessed little appreciation for his identity. He chose to leave the household and pursue worldly gratification, although his royal identity never left him. After he reaped the consequences of his wanderings and debauchery, he found himself living off leftovers in the hog yard. That's where he had a realization of who he actually was: royalty.

This identity was intact, though he was in perhaps the most demeaning position a person can be in and starving. "Even my father's servants have enough to spare, and I'm here perishing with hunger," he said to himself. (See verse 17.) This glimmer of identity was enough to stir his faith and propel him out of the mud and onto the road back home. He was becoming hungry for who he was and tired of who he wasn't.

When the son got home, his father did something amazing. Looking past his son's prepared apology, he completely restored the former prodigal on the spot, giving him the tools and symbols of authority: robe, shoes, and ring. We will return to this aspect of the story later, but what happens next throws great light on the son who now realized his royalty and the one who didn't. You see, the prodigal son had an older brother whose journey was not as beneficial.

This elder brother lived in his father's household and served faithfully (at least by his own description), but he had no revelation of royalty. He was a poor man in a rich family. This perfectly describes so many Christians today. They are in the family of God but not experiencing the benefits of their royal identity. They actually remain in lack in the wealthiest household imaginable!

The prodigal son had progressed in the revelation of his identity. He attained the provision and standing of his identity by coming into agreement with his self-image (with his father's generous help). The elder brother, however, remained in a begging, toiling mindset. Because he had not gained the revelation of his royalty, he lived like a servant, complaining that his father had never given him a goat for a feast, when in fact the fixings for a feast were in the fridge all along!

We might call this the parable of the revelation of royalty. Donald Lawrence, a gifted musician, used to come to our church and sing about restoring your righteous mind. That is exactly what this parable shows. The prodigal progressed in revelation of his identity. The elder brother did not. In the same way, some believers progress in their revelation of identity, and some choose not to.

Born Into the Palace

Of course, there are some people who want to live with all the kingdom benefits without truly being born again. They try to take steps 2, 3, 4, and 5 without starting with step 1—saying yes to Jesus and their identity as a child of God. To walk in our royalty, we must be born again into the royal family. For the prodigal, I would say this happened when he was in the hog yard. Salvation, which requires repentance, is the first step to gaining the kingdom and walking in the reality of your royalty.

For me, this happened when I worked in computer sales at IBM in Chicago. An administrator at IBM invited me to go out with her, and I wasn't married at the time so I saw it as an opportunity for a date. But when I asked where she wanted to go, she said mysteriously, "I'll take you somewhere." I agreed to go, assuming we were going to a club.

She took me somewhere, all right—to a church meeting! Little did I know she was a charismatic Catholic. We pulled into a schoolyard and entered the back door of an auditorium. People were singing and raising their hands. This certainly was not a club! Yet that night became the turning point of my life. I heard the words of the speaker, and the gospel hit home. I gave my life to the Lord, and everything went to another level. I was empowered in so many ways. I had taken step 1.

When you take step 1, you are born out of the womb of the Holy Ghost. You come alive spiritually. Like the once-prodigal son, you apprehend every bit of royalty you will ever possess because all of your identity is realized at once. It takes time to walk in the image of God—as Paul says, we are changed from glory to glory—but our entrance into the household is secure. We find ourselves immediately walking in the good works that He ordained for us before the foundation of the world—works we can do only with God's ability.

Only those who have embraced and accepted their royal identity can walk in the assignments and power of the King, as the once-prodigal son now walked in royal shoes. The Father gives His shoes, robe, and ring only to those who operate in His nature of love, peace, joy, long-suffering, and other kingdom characteristics.

YE ARE GODS

The Bible says something truly out of this world that many people overlook or avoid because they have not understood it. You find it in Psalm 82, where the Bible states plainly: "I have said, Ye are gods; and all of you are children of the most High" (v. 6).

The "ye" He speaks to here is indicated in verse 1, which says, "God standeth in the congregation of the mighty; he judgeth among the gods." God was not talking to Himself, the Son, or the Holy Ghost. He was talking to His offspring, which is you and me. Acts 17:29 affirms this description when it says, "Forasmuch then as we are the offspring of God."

Many pastors and Bible teachers shy away from teaching this reality for fear that some in their congregations will take it the wrong way and fall into pride. Others simply don't understand the kingdom of God and our position in it. As a result, their congregations remain confused about their identity.

Let's be clear: mankind is not sovereign or all-powerful. There is only one God and one Lord and Savior, Jesus Christ, who suffered, died, and was raised from the dead so we could be reunited with the Father. But it was Jesus Himself who quoted these very words from Psalm 82 in a confrontation with religious leaders in the temple in Jerusalem.

> The Jews who were there gathered around him,
> saying, "How long will you keep us in suspense?
> If you are the Messiah, tell us plainly." Jesus
> answered, "I did tell you, but you do not believe....
> Is it not written in your Law, 'I have said you are
> "gods"'? If he called them 'gods,' to whom the word
> of God came—and Scripture cannot be set aside—
> what about the one whom the Father set apart as
> his very own and sent into the world? Why then do
> you accuse me of blasphemy because I said, 'I am
> God's Son'?"
>
> —JOHN 10:24–25, 34–36, NIV

God wants you to know that Christ is in you, "the hope of glory" (Col. 1:27), which is an expression of your full potential in Him. Satan fights this revelation tooth and nail because unless you see yourself in the God class, as the late evangelist T. L. Osborn said, it is difficult for you to receive the precious things God has for you. Your inheritance comes only in proportion to your new identity.

We must draw our identity from the Bible, not the media or the culture we live in. We must study the Scriptures to learn who God says we are. And whoever He says we are, that's who we are! God's Word cannot be broken or changed. Friend, "ye are gods." People may want to stone you for declaring this revelation, but God doesn't have any problem with it. He's the One who said, "Let us make man in our image, after our likeness" (Gen. 1:26). God knows we will never be God with a capital g. But He made us to be in the God class, which is why He calls us "gods."

How much you believe this will determine how much you manifest the power of this reality. Your image sets the limits on how much God can work through you. You have to believe that you have what it takes to manifest what God is leading you to do. Remember, we are called "believers," not "doubters"! Mark 9:23 says, "If thou canst believe, all things are possible to him that believeth." Jesus elsewhere said, "He who believes in Me, the works that I do he will do also; and greater works than these he will do, because I go to My Father" (John 14:12, NKJV).

I believe part of these "greater works" includes eradicating poverty, stopping the violence in our urban neighborhoods, restoring the lives of the formerly imprisoned, and rebuilding our communities and cities so they become a Garden of Eden. Only through God's superior kingdom and His supernatural power can this level of transformation take place, a transformation that leaves no trace of the previous conditions caused by the curse or even by our mistakes.

But so many people stand there with their feet rooted to the ground, refusing to walk down kingdom paths.

WE ARE GOD'S GOVERNORS

A major problem in God's family is the number of people who become born again but won't move ahead in God's purposes for them. Salvation, as priceless as it is, is just the entryway into the Father's house. The purpose isn't to hang around just inside the door. You can't receive an inheritance in the foyer. Jesus said that in His Father's house are many mansions. He wants us to run in and explore the rest of the house! He wants us to check out every room on every floor, every corner, every fixture and piece of furniture. Why? Because we own it with Him!

In the prodigal son parable, when the wandering son returned home with a repentant heart, people filled the house with feasting, preparation, and celebration. They owned the place, so to speak. They felt comfortable there, empowered, free to celebrate and serve. That is our calling as well. Many believers stall at the front door and somehow become convinced that salvation is the only thing they have gained and that their greatest challenge is to stay saved until they go to heaven. How tragic! Being born again to your revelation of royalty is just the beginning of your lifestyle of living in the promises here on the earth. You are supposed to get all the promises of Dad's house!

If there were a part 2 to the prodigal son parable (and perhaps in heaven there is), I have no doubt it would show the younger son ruling and reigning over his father's estate. Why do we know this? Because his father gave him the royal robe and ring, signaling it was time for him to implement the father's will over the father's realm. Having realized and understood his royalty, the younger son was prepared to rule well, while the older son still had lessons to learn to get him out of a toiling, begging, deprived mindset. This is an amazing parable about your identity and what happens to you when you have a revelation of royalty and insist on your true identity. We all should aspire to be like the once-prodigal son.

What God's Government Looks Like

Proverbs 8 assures us that by wisdom kings rule and rulers decree justice (v. 15). When a king or queen's image is right, the wisdom of God pours through his or her decision-making. Every king and queen, ruler and lord must operate in wisdom. God will not pour through a person with a bad self-image, or the decisions themselves will be tainted and unjust. The prophet Isaiah describes the kind of government Jesus would establish, and we would administer, on the earth:

> For unto us a child is born, unto us a son is given: and the government shall be upon his shoulder: and his name shall be called Wonderful, Counsellor, The mighty God, The everlasting Father, The Prince of Peace. Of the increase of his government and peace there shall be no end.
>
> —Isaiah 9:6–7

God's government is described here as wonderful, full of perfect counsel, mighty, everlasting, full of peace, ever-increasing. That's because the King Himself is wonderful, full of perfect counsel, mighty, everlasting, and full of peace. When we see Him for who He is, we see ourselves for who He made us to be. Our images align, and we govern in these ways.

This is why Jesus told us to pray, "Thy kingdom come, Thy will be done in earth, as it is in heaven" (Matt. 6:10). He was reaffirming the very thing God spoke in Genesis 1:28 when He created Adam and Eve: "And God blessed them, and God said unto them, Be fruitful, and multiply, and replenish the earth, and subdue it." His plan for humanity has never changed. Establishing His kingdom is even the basis of our prayer life, according to Jesus.

Our purpose as the church is to bring God's government into authority upon the earth. This government of God is more powerful than any other government that has existed or will ever exist. It is time for believers to rise into their identity of royalty and govern extraordinarily in every sphere of society. It is time for the church to finish what Adam started and operate in the fruitful dominion of the kingdom of God here and now.

CHAPTER 3

ENEMIES OF ROYALTY

B EFORE WE LOOK further at how we function within the government of God, let's glance for a moment at the opposition's tactics—specifically at the kingdom of darkness the enemy is trying to build on the earth.

Satan's evil kingdom is based on the opposite values of God's kingdom. You can flip each heavenly principle on its head and get an accurate picture of what Satan wants. Unfortunately, many believers actually choose to remain enslaved to this dark kingdom even after they become born again. But you don't have to live in that dark kingdom anymore! Let's expose Satan's principles so we can eradicate his influence on our royal revelation.

SATAN'S KINGDOM OF SLAVES

While God's kingdom operates on perfect principles of love, joy, peace, patience, integrity, royal demeanor, heavenly provision, and much more, Satan's kingdom operates on lower principles such as lying, cheating, revenge, hatred, abuse, and other inferior, degrading principles.

These principles do not build up but tear down and keep people trapped in feelings of chaos and fear. Demons work to create environments that reinforce Satan's power at the expense of God's royal children and basic human dignity.

Unfortunately, some born-again people observe the ways of "successful" unsaved people, read their books, and emulate their practices. The problem is that these tactics often include wicked forms of manipulation, self-promotion, and so forth. Satan's ways (which are the world's ways) never build the government of God's kingdom. They are totally ineffective, inferior, and counterproductive. "What partnership has light with Belial?" Paul asked. (See 2 Corinthians 6:15.) For this reason, Proverbs 14:12 instructs us that there is a way that seems right but leads to destruction. People who function under Satan's principles may prosper in the short term, but the long-term effects are always destructive. That is Satan's goal—to destroy (John 10:10).

How does our enemy do this? He always starts with your image.

INFERIORITY IMAGE

The basic belief Satan tries to instill in all people, especially God's children, is a mindset or image of inferiority, which is the opposite of royalty. Image inferiority causes the child of God not to see and embrace his or her true image, and it cuts God's children off from their inheritance. A mindset or image of inferiority empowers all harmful behaviors and beliefs that follow in its terrible path.

To suffer from an inferiority image simply means you feel lower in status, lesser in value, lagging in provision and protection. Psychologists often use the phrase *inferiority complex*—personal feelings of inadequacy or a belief that one is deficient compared to others. It is a lie that, when believed, blocks powerful truth from working in your life.

An image inferiority can look different in different people. Some hang their heads and keep their eyes low, manifesting the self-hatred Satan whispers to them. Others have the opposite reaction and try to exalt themselves or speak boastfully to cover feelings of shame or inadequacy. Some become overly sensitive to criticism, while others seem to invite criticism and accept harsh or abusive remarks because it confirms their supposed inferiority. There is no single, obvious flaw we see in those who suffer from an inferiority image. Manifestations can take many forms.

Even the great leader Moses suffered from an inferiority image. This image caused Moses to try to convince God that he was not the right person to go before Pharaoh and set his people free. "O my LORD, I am not eloquent, neither heretofore, nor since thou hast spoken unto thy servant: but I am slow of speech, and of a slow tongue," Moses said, arguing with God based on Moses' feeling of inferiority. God answered, "Who hath made man's mouth?" (Exod. 4:10–11). In other words, God was saying, "Don't degrade what I have exalted. Don't make inferior what I have made superior. I made man, and I made your mouth. I know how powerful it is and how I'm going to use it to release an entire nation from

29

slavery." God knows the value of everything in creation. He never sells us short of our royal image. Who made you? God did!

Many children of God today need to be set free from the bondage of an inferiority image. Just like with the children of Israel in the land of Egypt, the enemy has convinced many royal children that they are slaves though they are not. All he needs is your agreement, which is why he works hard to persuade each of us of our lowliness and lack. He whittles away at our image to get us to agree with his false claims. "Oh, this is as good as I'll ever be," someone might say. "I guess I'm not meant for great things. I'll always come up short. I'm just trying to get by." That's devil-talk, not God-talk.

Brother, sister, you and I were born into the palace! "Ye are gods." Our Father is the King! We are full-fledged members of the royal family, a new race of rulers on the earth. We are part of a new royal dynasty here to expose a new dimension to the world, because once they see it, they will want to be a part of it. God gives only as a King gives—the biggest and the best—and He teaches us to give that same way.

We can't submit to any thought lower than our actual status. Such ideas are beneath our attention. We must instead listen to our Mentor and Teacher, the Holy Ghost, who helps us reach our destinies. When we give the enemy ground by denying our true image, the Holy Ghost quickly says, "No, don't talk like that. That's not the way a king should talk." He points us to the hundreds of places in the Bible that reveal and celebrate our royal heritage. "You are the righteousness of God, the seed of Abraham, and not inferior to anyone," He tells us.

He works constantly to get us to live above the line.

LIVING ABOVE THE LINE

The enemy tries to pull our image below its true level, to get us living below the line. What do I mean? A preacher-friend of mine refers to what he calls the "light line." Everything below that line is temporal. It is based on human logic and reason and an inferior image built on the natural realm. However, everything above the light line is in God's royal realm of total provision and empowerment. Above the line, you're dealing with eternity; below the line, you're in the enemy's temporal grip, stuck in an inferiority image, confined to the sensory realm. Below the line is all toil and confusion, sweat, exertion, hopelessness, and fatigue. It is a place of guesswork and uncertainty, trial and error, an "I hope this works" attitude. There is nothing royal about it.

Let me give one example of someone I knew who lived below the line. Some time ago, a preacher-friend (different from the one I just referenced) called me and shared that an unsaved man called him and said, "Something told me to give you my house, and I am to take your house." My friend ignored the man because he thought it was a prank.

But two weeks or so later, the man called again, this time in a panic.

"I am here in Las Vegas," the man said excitedly on the phone, "and something told me, 'Get up and give that man your house!'"

So my friend agreed to come see the house. As he pulled up to the gate, he could see the property was huge. The owner was waiting for him on the porch about 150 yards further from the gate. Arriving at the house, he glanced behind the man and saw a waterfall flowing over onyx stones inside the house. The whole place was magnificent.

The owner took my friend on a tour of the house and concluded by saying, "All we need to do is go to the title office. You give me your house, and I'll give you this one. Are you ready to go?"

My friend said he paused and said, "I don't know. How much is the water bill?"

That is a below-the-line mindset! The unsaved owner actually had to put pressure on my friend to get him to accept that beautiful house. Why? Because my friend was used to living below the line. In his mind, his status was too low, his income not enough to make it all work. More than that, he simply didn't see himself as the kind of person who would own such a wonderful house.

He didn't realize that as believers, we were not born here but born from above (John 3:3). We were born to do supernatural things like create, possess, and rule.

ON A BOAT BELOW THE LINE

When people operate below the line, all they can deal with is what is seen. But it takes spiritual sight to make a real change in this world. The spiritual realm is meant to control the natural realm, not the other way around. Natural cannot change natural. It can only rearrange it.

One night the disciples of Jesus were in a boat with

Him when a storm came up. Their below-the-line thinking saw only the natural occurrence. As experienced fishermen, they knew in the natural that this was one of those storms that sunk boats. They panicked and probably tried everything they could in the natural to bail out water as it flooded the craft. However, this storm was actually spiritual: Satan had launched an attack that human efforts could not compete with. Natural energy would never overcome it. Thankfully, they had someone in the boat who was living above the line.

Jesus was asleep in the stern when the disciples woke Him up—and they even accused Him of disinterest, based on their natural thinking! "Don't you care that we're going to drown?" (Mark 4:38, NLT). He didn't allow their unwise, unfounded accusations to push Him off course. He could have argued with them and reminded them of the amazing miracles He had just performed. But Jesus overlooked their insult because arguing, complaining, and strife are all below the line. Their natural reaction didn't need to impede His progress.

He spoke to the wind and the sea and instantly produced a great calm. Remember, only the spiritual can control the natural. Above the line is royal authority; below the line are problems and powerlessness. Jesus then looked at His natural-thinking followers and said, "Where is your faith?" (See Mark 4:40.) He meant that they could have lived above the line and done the exact same thing He did! The disciples were of the royal family, just like you and me. They had the God-given ability to take authority over the storm by faith and expect the same results Jesus got.

Jesus said, "The works that I do shall he do also; and greater works than these shall he do" (John 14:12). You see, there are no improbabilities or impossibilities above the line. With God, all things are possible.

THE FEARLESS PLACE

Fear cannot prevail over you above the line. Once a person realizes that God can neither lie (Titus 1:2) nor fail, he or she can rest assured that He always keeps His Word.

Fear usually begins with a natural thought dressed up like a fact. A below-the-line idea sneaks above the line and tries to ensnare you. That's what happened with the disciples in the storm. They knew from past natural experience that such storms were deadly. They just didn't consider that now they were living above the line rather than below it. Reality was different for them now.

When fear enters as a thought, it quickly grows into a way of thinking. It builds scaffolding and foundations to support itself and justify its existence. Our minds are wired to go in the direction of our most dominant thoughts. Whatever we meditate on grows and becomes more convincing to us over time. Below-the-line thoughts based in fear, doubt, and natural experience become mental strongholds.

Think of it like a snake attack. There are two different strategies snakes use to subdue their prey. One type of snake strikes with a venomous bite that paralyzes its victim with poison. Then the snake can consume it. A nonvenomous snake like a boa constrictor, the largest snake in the world, squeezes the life out of its prey. It strategically tightens whenever its prey exhales. In both cases, the victim is paralyzed and consumed.

The devil uses "poison" and "constriction" to paralyze and suffocate. Fear is like a poison and a vise. Its deadly effect spreads toxic thoughts and emotions through our systems and makes us feel we are suffocating, slowing down, and giving in. Some people feel this when they board a plane, step in front of a group to speak, encounter a certain person, or receive a certain type of phone call or email. Fear attempts to use natural, below-the-line means to cause people to meditate on threats that don't actually exist. Someone may believe, "I'm going to die from the same thing my mother did." The enemy uses that thought as an inroad to work a person over and drag him or her further below the light line. It even worked on the first human, Adam. When God called to him, Adam responded, "I was afraid" (Gen. 3:10). Fear was part of the fall of humanity.

Fear not only affects individuals but also has the power to paralyze an entire nation. A spirit of fear caused the children of Israel to question the righteous report of Joshua and Caleb about the Promised Land. They instead believed the fear-filled report of the other ten spies, which warped their judgment. They actually concluded that Moses, Joshua, and Caleb were their enemies! They plotted among themselves and said, "Let us appoint a new leader because the one we have is leading us to be slaughtered by the giants in Canaan land." (See Numbers 14:3–4.) Fear causes you to misjudge everything—a situation, a circumstance, a person, and God.

You will see the friend who is helping you as someone trying to hurt you.

This is the blinding effect of fear. This is why the prophet Elisha prayed for his servant Gehazi, "LORD, I pray thee, open his eyes, that he may see" (2 Kings 6:17), when the Syrian army surrounded their town. When Gehazi's eyes were opened to see the chariots of fire (angels), his fear disappeared.

When we live below the line, we lose our vision of reality. People who are unable to see move slowly and tentatively in unfamiliar environments. They can't make bold moves based on what they see. Fear blocks your vision, stops your progress, and keeps you living far beneath your royal privileges.

LACK OF KNOWLEDGE

Some folks are not afraid but simply ignorant. This is not a put-down. To be ignorant is to lack knowledge about something.

To be truly ignorant is to not even realize you are ignorant. Many people think they know everything they need to know, but their lives don't show the best results. I'm here to tell you that if you've been on the road to a certain destination for forty years and haven't gotten there yet, maybe you don't actually know where you're going! Maybe you've got the wrong map and are on the wrong road. It's time to pull over and get some knowledge—to free yourself from ignorance.

The enemy is constantly plotting to shake you and rob you of revelation knowledge. Whenever revelation comes, he is waiting nearby to steal it. Jesus said in a parable in Mark 4 that the enemy comes in five ways (vv. 15–19):

1. Affliction

2. Persecution

3. The cares of this world

4. Deceitfulness of riches

5. Lust for other things

Anytime you go to church or a meeting and get a good word, the devil immediately tries to come and snatch it up. He will use anybody and anything to do it—family, friends, coworkers, or the media. He knows that when God's Word takes root, it changes your inner image, and when your image is changed, nothing can stop you from receiving from God.

This is why Jesus gave us a marker to determine whether or not we are ignorant. He said, "Wisdom is known by her children." (See Matthew 11:19.) If the kingdom is not manifesting in your life, perhaps you just don't know enough or you have a wrong understanding of your royalty. If that is the case, then the Word of God becomes a theology but not a life-changing revelation. Isaiah 5:13 says, "Therefore my people are gone into captivity, because they have no knowledge." Hosea 4:6 says, "My people are destroyed for lack of knowledge." This knowledge is not head knowledge but revelation knowledge, not academic theory but heavenly illumination.

The Bible says knowledge comes easily to a man of understanding (Prov. 1:5). This refers to life above the line. The place of understanding is above the line. To be a man or a woman of understanding simply means rising to a revelation of your royalty. There you can see and receive revelation of everything you need to know.

SACRED COWS

Sometimes the problem is not what we lack but what is inside of us (i.e., wrong belief systems) as we step into our Father's house.

It's amazing how the Israelites left Egypt behind—but took Egypt inside of them. When they were encamped in the wilderness waiting for Moses to come down from meeting with God, they convinced Aaron, Moses' brother, to make them a golden calf. This was the original sacred cow, and of course there was nothing sacred about it. It was as unholy as you could get.

This idol was made out of gold. Where did this precious metal come from? From Egypt! Remember that the Israelites had despoiled (stripped) Egypt when God caused the Egyptian people to give their precious jewelry and clothing to the departing nation. Now God's people used those very blessings to create an abomination.

Sacred cows often exist inside of us and accompany us wherever we go. People bring these cows into marriages, new jobs, churches, and elsewhere. These cows are idols that people worship outside the plan of God. They become belief systems—strongholds—that people are very reluctant to give up.

I brought such a sacred cow into my marriage, and it almost ruined us.

MY MARRIAGE

About six months after I married my wife, Veronica, the honeymoon phase wore off and I started looking at her funny. I became very critical and began to wonder if the Lord really had told me to marry her. The enemy was busy planting thoughts in my mind: "She can't cook like she said she could. You thought she had this together and that together. But she ain't got it together. See, you married the wrong woman." These thoughts crowded my mind even though my wife was and is a very wonderful woman. I started trying to figure out how I was going to get out of the marriage.

You see, some things that I had witnessed between my mother and father as a young boy growing up had negatively shaped my view of marriage. My parents eventually divorced, and some things they said influenced my thinking. Words paint pictures inside of us that influence what we see and how we act—and react—in life. Pictures like this do not go away until we replace them with God's truth. I was about to understand I had a problem, and it was not my wife.

In the middle of this crisis, one night I attended a meeting where a man was teaching about confession and how ungodly thoughts can reside in our lives and we may not even know it. These ideas can actually control our minds when we live out of an incorrect image. The minister said, "Start confessing God's Word over your spouse." That statement impacted me.

I took him at his word, came home, and started reading his book, *Praying God's Word*. I began confessing God's Word over my wife, drawing from Proverbs 31: "My wife is a virtuous woman. She always does me good as long as there is life within her. The bread of idleness, discontent, and self-pity she does not eat. She gets up early and gets spiritual food for the house. She assigns her maids to their tasks. She does not neglect her present duties by assuming others. I thank You that she loves me. She admires me exceedingly, and the Word is working mightily in our marriage. We have been transformed into the image of Jesus by the renewing of our minds. I thank You that my wife is a wife of the Word. She is a woman of the Word, and wisdom is flowing from her lips."

Every day I confessed this. When I first began, I thought I was saying it for my wife. Eventually I figured out I was saying it for me! I was the one who needed to change. The confession changed my image, and I began to act differently. I found out that you cannot move any further than your image. If your image is a bad marriage, then that is the direction you will move. Once I got my image straightened out, I began to see and act differently. I had judged my current situation based on my past experience, but I had poor judgment rooted in fear. All of that began to change as I confessed the truth about my wife. The image of my marriage began to change.

Because of my confession, today my marriage is made in heaven. I even sit up at night thinking about how I can bless my wife more and more. This is the same marriage the devil told me I should leave! If I had changed wives before I had changed this distorted image, Satan would have gotten the best of me with the same trick again and again. My negative confession was a sacred cow within me, something I didn't think to distrust until that man's message challenged me to look at it differently. This is why *biblical meditation* is so important in changing ungodly mindsets and images. I call it the *missing link of meditation* in the body of Christ.

In the same way, Aaron and the Israelites made a "sacred" cow and began dancing lewdly around it. It greatly angered God, who had Moses crush it, mix it in water, and make the people drink it. Maybe it tasted horribly bitter, or maybe it was a laxative—I don't know! But the result must have been strong if the purpose was to destroy that idol once and for all and change the way God's people thought.

COMPROMISES AND BARGAINS

Another mistake God's children make is to enter into compromise or agreement with the enemy. When Moses told Pharaoh to let God's people go, Pharaoh tried to negotiate terms and conditions. Pharaoh told Moses, "Go, worship the LORD. Even your women and children may go with you; only leave your flocks and herds behind" (Exod. 10:24, NIV). Moses said, "No! I'm not going to do that."

God does not give us permission to compromise our revelation of royalty. You can't barter it away or wash it off. It's on you for life. Whether or not you benefit from it depends on the knowledge you have and choose to act on. But the enemy cannot change your identity. Neither can you.

Here's the only bargain you are allowed to make with the devil: he has to pay back sevenfold everything he stole from you when you were below the line! When you

41

got saved, everything you were entitled to from God's Word came with salvation, and everything Satan did against you, he must repay sevenfold. The Bible calls this recompense. Jesus paid for it through His redemptive work on the cross. This means it doesn't make a difference even if you made the mistake. The devil still has to pay you back handsomely. Our Father the King defends His children well.

A People Living Above the Line

Above the line is a place of no compromise and no limitation. Jesus said the things He did we shall do also. Was Jesus a world changer? Yes, and so are you! We are made in His image. We can use our faith to speak the wisdom and will of God over a community and change it for kingdom glory. The church should be out front of every generation. God has set up a supernatural system designed to surpass any results that can be achieved by operating in the world's system. The revelation of royalty and walking by faith are the dividing line between the possible and the impossible.

Let me ask you, Are you living above the line?

Above the line there are no financial impossibilities. You have funds to solve any problem. Why? Because in God the answer is always there before the problem manifests. The devil caused the problem—and God was there before the devil. Operating above the line is a whole other realm, where you flow differently than you do in the natural realm.

With God's wisdom and spiritual discernment, you will start to recognize everything in your environment as an opportunity for restoration and improvement through your royal exercise of wisdom and authority. You will not have to struggle to believe you are the righteous child of a miracle-working God. You were made for signs, wonders, and miracles. (See Isaiah 8:18.) When you wake up in the morning, you say, "I am blessed all day today. I am blessed going to work this morning, and I'm blessed coming home. I am blessed when I rise and when I lie down. I am blessed in the city and in the field—wherever I go and whatever I do."

Remember, you and I are in the God class. We are the righteousness of God. We have been given the same attributes as our Father. When you live above the line, you won't be able to stop yourself from growing in anointing, authority, position, and power. You won't be able to stop the innovations and improvements from pouring through you. You will see how easy it is to take even a city for God. Like the early church in Acts 17:6, you and I will turn this world upside down.

Brother or sister, hold fast to the confession of your identity and image. Stay above the line. Don't let the devil convince you to compromise, overwhelm you with fear, or otherwise drag you back below the line into the natural realm. We have been ordained, as Esther was, for such a time as this. God is ready to take us further than any of us have ever gone. He loves to see us exercising our dominion mandate throughout the earth.

So start acting like you're in charge here, because as kings and queens in the government of God, we are!

CHAPTER 4

DECLARING YOUR ROYALTY OUT LOUD

⸺✦⸺⸺⸺⸺⸺⸺⸺✦⸺

AS KINGS AND queens, we comport ourselves differently. We behave according to royal protocols that enhance and magnify the glory of our position and authority. Some things are beneath us as royalty, and we must learn what these are. As the Holy Spirit does His job of bringing out the king or queen in us, He teaches us a royal way of walking, talking, believing, thinking, and behaving that is entirely fitting for children of the King on the earth.

Perhaps the biggest aspect of this is our words.

THE MOST POWERFUL THING ON EARTH

One of the first skills the Holy Spirit teaches us is how to speak. Just as a young child learns to form words and sentences that help him or her to navigate life and exercise authority in small ways and then big ones, so God's royal children are on a journey of learning to speak kingdom words. In the natural realm, speaking sets humans apart from all other creatures. Words and complex communication are a major part of what makes us more powerful than other earthly beings. In the realm of the kingdom of God, too, words carry more power than anything else. They build up and destroy, establish and fulfill, heal, kill, and raise from death. God demonstrated this by literally speaking the universe into existence. Jesus Himself is called "the Word...made flesh" (John 1:14). God has exalted His name and His word above all things! There is nothing higher.

As children of God, you and I have the power to speak words that impact everything on earth. Your words set the course of your life, your business, your relationships, and your destiny. Even the corrupt world system has speech protocols. As people ascend the corporate ladder, their words and conversations change because their words carry greater impact. If they say one wrong thing, it could cause trouble for the whole corporation and many lives. This is why God's royal children must learn to speak royal words.

The Bible gives us many promises to encourage us to grow in this area. Job 22:28 says, "Thou shalt also decree a thing, and it shall be established unto thee." The Lord said through the prophet Isaiah, "So shall my word be that goeth forth out of my mouth: it shall not return unto me void, but it shall accomplish that which I please" (Isa. 55:11). And Numbers 23:19 says, "Has He spoken, and will He not make it good?" (NKJV).

Even salvation comes through words: "If thou shalt confess with thy mouth the Lord Jesus, and shalt believe in thine heart that God hath raised him from the dead, thou shalt be saved" (Rom. 10:9).

Mary the mother of Jesus received nothing more than a word from God, which she believed and which was fulfilled (Luke 1:26–38). Jesus said, "Assuredly, I say to you, whatever you bind on earth will be bound in heaven, and whatever you loose on earth will be loosed in heaven" (Matt. 18:18, NKJV). Ninety-nine percent of what Jesus accomplished in His three-year ministry on earth He accomplished with words. He was demonstrating that spoken words are the way kings and queens get things done. They are how you will reach your highest potential and fulfill your God-given assignments. Ours is a word-ruled planet. It was created with words, and it is maintained by words. This is our assignment.

Of course, we know that Adam fell and his words changed. Instead of naming animals and powerfully proclaiming manifestations of kingdom creativity, his mouth became full of unholy fear and blame. His words started going in reverse, damaging the earth and destroying his destiny. His words remained powerful but were now destructive rather than constructive. Your words and mine are the same way—exceptionally powerful for whatever purpose we put them to.

Because the royal assignment of humanity has never changed, the Holy Spirit and angels are still waiting to act on words that agree with what God has already spoken about our situations and circumstances. When our words agree with His, transformational power flows. This is the primary exercise of our royalty.

SPEAKING BY FAITH

Words alone possess no power. Jesus said some unrighteous people believe they are heard "because of their
many words" (Matt. 6:7, NIV). But those are faithless,
powerless words. To possess power, words must be
spoken in faith in agreement with God's will.

Faith is the currency of the kingdom, and anything
we receive will be received by faith. It takes faith to be
saved, faith to be healed, and faith to access anything
else we need or desire from God. In Acts 3:12 and 16,
Peter said to the people who had witnessed the lame man
being healed, "Why look ye so earnestly on us, as though
by our own power or holiness we had made this man to
walk?...His name through faith in his name hath made
this man strong." Words spoken by faith in the name of
Jesus bring results. Faith alone won't work, and words
alone won't work. But together they are the most powerful combination in the created order.

God gives us a word for anything we need or desire in
life. Just as God calls invisible things into being, so do
we. We are made to walk just like God and talk just like
God, who "calleth those things which be not as though
they were" (Rom. 4:17). We are made to see just like
God, looking not at the things that are seen but at the
things that are not seen. If we say and do what God gives
us to say and do, then God will fulfill what He has promised. God's Word never returns to Him void, and He is
not a man that He should (or could) lie. His Word assures
us, "So then faith cometh by hearing, and hearing by the
word of God" (Rom. 10:17).

Speaking faith-filled words overrides the curse of

disease, sickness, poverty, oppression, broken relationships, and failing government systems. Faith-filled words cure communities, heal broken hearts, mend relationships, and establish nationwide prosperity. Faith-filled words fuel families, inspire individuals, and catapult churches into new realms of effective ministry. Faith-filled words can overrule and overcome anything in your life and open channels for divine favor to flow through you, producing prosperity in every area. Whatever issues you might have in your family, business, church, or community, words spoken by faith are designed to improve them.

LEGISLATING YOUR SUCCESS

Words are the means by which we legislate royal realities into existence in earthly realms. Royalty literally legislates God's kingdom on earth by God-given words spoken in faith. We "decree a thing" by faith, and it comes to pass (Job 22:28). A decree is "an order usually having the force of law."[1] It is used to legislate. Words don't just express opinions; they establish realities, change destinies, and call forth invisibilities. Words allow God's power to flow through us in proportion to the image of God in us. Like God, we decree words of life in the midst of seemingly impossible and catastrophic situations, transforming those situations by the power of His Word.

When I left my well-paying job at IBM to attend seminary at Oral Roberts University (I'll say more about that journey later), Veronica and I found ourselves at a lower place financially for a time. We weren't enjoying the finer things of life, unless you consider bologna sandwiches high cuisine!

One day at the beginning of the school year, our class met in the chapel to pray. I didn't know why we were there, but we started praying in the Spirit, and suddenly everything got quiet. I could tell that one particular student had a prophetic anointing, and he came over to me and said, "I don't know who you are, but you are the beginning of a new line of wealth."

That was very encouraging to Veronica and me, and we both felt provoked to walk in obedience to this word. Like me, Veronica had worked at IBM before we moved, and she desired to work again, so she started looking for a local job in computers. The initial results seemed discouraging. She visited local employment agencies, and they told her no one was hiring. In fact, they said, companies were laying off hundreds of people. We knew this was an evil report—a faithless word—meant to be overcome, so we decided not to let circumstances govern us but rather to legislate our circumstances with words. Veronica got out a set of index cards, and together we designed her perfect job. We wrote down each aspect of it:

- She wanted to work in computers.

- She wanted a job no more than ten minutes from our house.

- She wanted to work in a nice office.

- She wanted a certain salary.

- She wanted a company car.

Then Veronica went to the Bible and found scriptures that agreed with what she desired. She wrote those down and taped them up all over the house. I would look at a window and see a card that read, "My God shall supply all my needs according to His riches in glory." I would open the refrigerator and see a card that read, "I am redeemed from the curse." Everywhere I went, these faith words stood before me, and together Veronica and I came into agreement for this job to materialize. No longer were we focusing on the problem or the bad report. We had turned our focus to the answer because we were sure that God's Word spoken in faith would deliver us from the problem.

When you focus your faith-filled words on problems, the enemy will try to test you. One day, a gentleman we knew came by the house to see me. Veronica was on the front lawn when he arrived, and on his way in he asked, "So, do you have your job yet?"

She said, "I sure do." She had not become employed yet, but to us the transaction had been accomplished in the Spirit. She was following biblical instructions to "hold fast the profession of our faith without wavering; (for he is faithful that promised;)" (Heb. 10:23). We knew that "faith is the substance of things hoped for, the evidence of things not seen" (Heb. 11:1).

This man asked, "Where is it?"

Veronica replied, "I don't know, but I got it."

It was a bold thing to do in the face of skepticism and the man's "show me" approach to life. She saw firsthand how meditating on God's Word prepares you for moments like this. It takes courage and conviction to speak God's

51

promise to unbelieving people. Unfortunately, many people—even church folks—are not willing to do this. They are sensory-oriented as opposed to faith-oriented. They may say amen and hallelujah in church, but when pressure comes on them back home, they often say what the world system says. Like worldly people, they have to see, touch, hear, and feel what's happening before they believe it.

I'm here to tell you that faith works even when nothing seems to be happening. As you continue speaking and legislating your future, things begin to turn. You may not even notice the movement at first, but soon the momentum will carry you along in the direction of your words. This is because we have Jesus as our High Priest in heaven. He hears our words and is making sure we get what we have asked of the Father and confessed with our mouths. Once those faith-filled words are spoken, the Father immediately assigns angels to your case, and the Holy Spirit moves on your behalf. Your job and mine is to hold fast while the answer appears. This is exactly what my wonderful wife did.

Veronica could have been discouraged by the query of the man who came to see me. She might have responded, "Well, I don't have anything yet, and with the economy the way it is, it's not looking too good." All that seemed true to the natural mind—but we are designed to live above the line, as befits our royalty.

Shortly after that day, she got a call from the employment agency inviting her to consider interviewing for a job they had found. When she got home, we sat down with our index card and went down the list.

I said, "Is the job in computers?"

"Yes," she said, so we checked that off the list.

"How about ten minutes from the house?"

"Yes, it's about nine and a half," she said, so we checked that off the list.

"How about the money?"

"They are offering $5,000 more than what we put on the card," she replied.

We checked that one off.

"How about an automobile?"

"They told me to pick out a new Buick," she said.

Every one of those requests was fulfilled! I do believe that was the day we quit eating bologna sandwiches. Veronica started working in computers and bringing home good money while I attended seminary. She had made her way prosperous by following God's pattern and legislating her own success.

My friend, you were never designed to live in an environment you did not create. Words of faith are the tools God gives us to design our futures! It is the main way we as believers get things done on the earth.

SEEING AND DECREEING

Before we decree, we must first see. We cannot legislate what we have not looked upon within our spirits, because everything that manifests externally begins as an internally perceived reality. Or as one man of God said, everything is created twice—first in the spiritual realm and then in this physical world.

Consider this question: Where are the things that God speaks into existence before He speaks them? The answer is, they are in God. When He speaks them, He manifests them externally. We operate the same way—not from the outside in, but from the inside out. This is why Jesus said, "The kingdom of God is within you" (Luke 17:21). It is inside us, but it is not meant to stay inside of us! We speak it forth, and the kingdom manifests in the earth. Let me illustrate with a little story.

One afternoon, late in the day, I found myself getting hungry. So I went to the kitchen and looked in the refrigerator to see what might be on the menu for dinner. Although the refrigerator wasn't empty, I didn't see anything that looked like a meal. I went back into my study to finish working, and a very short time later Veronica called me to come out for dinner. I got to the table and was delightfully surprised by what I saw: a meal that looked like Thanksgiving dinner! But where had it come from?

I knew that Veronica hadn't gone out to the grocery store and that no one else had prepared the meal, so I asked her, "Where did all this food come from? When I checked the fridge earlier, I didn't see any of it."

"Oh, it was there," she said. "Some items were in the freezer and some in containers. We had plenty to eat."

We simply had a difference in what we saw. Veronica could see what I didn't see and knew that everything was there for a wonderful dinner. And it was, praise God!

I hope you see my point. The food existed inside the fridge, inside the freezer, and inside containers, and it was just a matter of manifesting it on the table as a hot meal. It went from internal to external, but it was always there. The Bible says, "By faith we understand that the worlds were framed by the word of God, so that the things which are seen were not made of things which are visible" (Heb. 11:3, NKJV). This is the very same principle. The world existed before it was visible—it was just inside of God at that time. *The Message* says it this way: "By faith, we see the world called into existence by God's word, what we see created by what we don't see."

Many people think God made the world out of nothing, but that is incorrect. He made the world out of what was invisible. I remember a popular R&B song in the seventies that said if you take nothing from nothing, you'll be left with nothing. The singer was making the point that a person needed to have something in order to be with him. That was a secular song with some profound spiritual truth in it!

God created the world from an invisible substance called faith. He saw it in the eternal realm and spoke it into existence: "And God said, Let there be light: and there was light" (Gen. 1:3).

It's worth repeating: God spoke what He saw, and what He saw came forth by what He said. Likewise we, as children of God, imitate our Father. (See Ephesians 5:1, NKJV.) We bring forth what we see by speaking in faith.

WRONG-TRACK WORDS

The enemy, of course, tries to restrain or hinder this exercise of power. His strategy is to control your power center—your words. He even tries to turn your words around so they become weapons you wield against yourself! Too many people fall for this trap. They think the devil is in charge and in control, but the Bible says death and life are not in the power of the devil but in the power of the tongue. We possess all the power!

The enemy's only chance is to persuade you to use your powerful weapon against yourself. The devil watches over your words, and once you release faithless words of death, disappointment, or discouragement, he has license to try to bring them to pass. In this way, many people legislate their own destruction. They poison their own potential. They pronounce failures on their own future.

The ten faithless Israelite spies gave an evil report after spying out Canaan and seeing the same things faithful Joshua and Caleb saw. People do not see *with* their eyes—they see *through* their eyes. The content of a person's heart shapes his or her worldview. This inner reality controls our external reality. The evil report manifested and became forty more years in the wilderness. They decreed it, and it was so. They exercised the power of the tongue to say, "Let there be."

Faith is the only way to stop the enemy from stopping you. If you are trying to transform a life, a company, a community, or a family, the enemy will try to turn your words into decrees of death rather than life-giving legislation from a place of royal rule.

Instead of saying, "I can't afford that," say, "With God, all things are possible."

Instead of saying, "I'm sick," say, "By His stripes, I am healed."

Instead of saying, "I'm weary," say, "The joy of the Lord is my strength."

Instead of saying, "I don't know how to get ahead," say, "God teaches me to prosper."

Instead of saying, "I'm lonely," say, "God said He'll never leave me nor forsake me."

Instead of saying, "I'm stuck in a terrible time," say, "Many are the afflictions of the righteous, but God will deliver me out of them all."

Then read your Bible and get that Word inside of you. Words stuck on a page will never assist you. They must be internalized and spoken by faith, which you can do at any time and throughout the day. Everyone knows that when you put God's Word inside of you, it begins to pour out in response to every situation. Just like Veronica responded to the man questioning her faith for a job, you will find your answer springing up from the invisible, powerful Word of God within you. Angels will flock to you when they hear you speak His Word, because the Bible says the angels hearken unto the voice of His word (Ps. 103:20). Your very mouth is what gives "voice" to His Word. This is one of the greatest realities of all.

I believe this is how Shadrach, Meshach, and Abednego were delivered from the fiery furnace in Daniel 3. Facing a death sentence because they refused to worship the king's golden idol, they said, "O Nebuchadnezzar...if it be so, our God whom we serve is able to deliver us from the burning fiery furnace, and he will deliver us out of thine hand, O king" (vv. 16–17).

The king became so furious that he commanded that the furnace be heated seven times hotter and had the young men thrown inside. But when the king looked in the furnace, he said, "Lo, I see four men loose, walking in the midst of the fire, and they have no hurt; and the form of the fourth is like the Son of God" (v. 25). When the king saw that "the fire had no power," he said, "Blessed be the God of Shadrach, Meshach, and Abednego, who hath sent his angel, and delivered his servants that trusted in him" (vv. 27–28).

Here's what happened: God sent His angel and delivered the three faithful men because of their words. They decreed a solution—"God whom we serve is able to deliver us from the burning fiery furnace, and he will deliver us out of thine hand"—and God sent His angel to respond to those words of faith. These men literally determined their result by the words they chose to speak, and so can you. Jesus said, "Your words now reflect your fate then: either you will be justified by them or you will be condemned" (Matt. 12:37, TLB).

ONLY GOD'S WORD MATTERS

Let me emphasize one thing: as royal governors in the King's court, our words must match His. We are rulers under the authority of the King of all kings. We are His ambassadors, sent to the earth to deliver His words and declare His realities into existence. In other words, we are people always speaking and acting under the authority of another.

The military taught me this foundational principle of spiritual leadership. I served in the US Air Force for a number of years, flying fighter jets in combat. I can assure you that I didn't fly a single mission unless I received orders from headquarters or from my commander. I didn't just take the jet out for a joyride. That would have been unthinkable! My decisions about where to go and what to do were not my own. I had to follow what we call the chain of command, and I had authority as long as I stayed under that authority. If I disobeyed or failed to follow my commander's orders, I could be court-martialed and sentenced to jail time or dishonorably discharged from the air force. Believe me, I stayed under authority!

During training, before taking off in our jets, we had to follow a flight checklist that monitored everything, including the barometric pressure, weight of the plane, gravitational pull, thrust applied, and so on. If I followed the checklist, I was guaranteed a successful takeoff. Once airborne, things worked the same way. The controller might say, "Bravo 66, turn right. Heading 360, maintain 3,000." In response you repeat back what they said. "Roger. Bravo 66 turning right, heading 360, maintaining 3,000." If you say exactly what the controller said and do what he said to do, everything is all right. You are under the chain of command.

God's kingdom functions the same way. God knows how to direct you. All you have to do is say what He says and follow His instructions. In the kingdom of God there are no opinions. Things are not up for a vote. We cannot choose the words and outcomes we want based on our whims and desires. Rather, our words must reflect His desires and established purposes. I like to say it this way: Jesus didn't come to make us comfortable; He came to make us conformable. He wants to conform, or mold, us into His image (Rom. 8:29). We have authority because we are people under authority.

I'm reminded of a time when my father gave me clear direction and I refused to follow it. I was a young boy, and he sent me to the barber for a haircut. Dad told me to have the barber cut it short, but I neglected to mention that. I came home, and my father looked at me sideways and asked, "Did you tell him to cut it all off?" I said, "No, I didn't."

Guess where I ended up? Back at the barber shop. My father made me go back and tell the barber to cut it all off! I had not carried out my father's word. I had to do that one over. I had to own my father's words and carry them out completely, letting his wishes be manifested on my head! You can't be under authority halfway. You must fully follow the words of your Father.

Ultimately, we must own our faith and live by it. One of the great faith passages in the Bible, Habakkuk 2:4, tells us, "The just shall live by his faith." We cannot live by someone else's faith—it must spring from within us. This is an important issue in the body of Christ. As I minister around the globe, it seems like faith is missing. Some people go to church because a relative goes there or for the good music or the exciting presentation. But what about faith? Shouldn't we go where our faith is growing?

Brother, sister—fellow heir of the King—let's legislate our success in His will by speaking words of faith in agreement with God's purposes. Then we will be operating in the greatest power in the universe.

PART II

A ROYAL REVELATION
⤜— IN MY —⤛
LIFE

CHAPTER 5

TUSKEGEE VISION

✦━━━━━━━━━✦

A FTER THE WORD of God and the work of the Holy Spirit in my life, the greatest contributor to my personal revelation of royalty came from the town I grew up in: Tuskegee, Alabama. Without even realizing it, I was trained in royalty, taught to live above the line, shown how to manifest internal realities, and made to feel like a royal son. It was an extraordinary atmosphere to be in.

Tuskegee was unique in the United States at that time. It was a hub of African American professionalism, innovation, education, creativity, medicine, and more. Many people have heard of the Tuskegee Airmen, a group of Black pilots who broke all sorts of color barriers and professional barriers in the mid-twentieth century. Many also have heard the name Booker T. Washington, who was the city's most important historical figure and really the architect of the city's royal vision. He started schools and industries, but more importantly he established a mindset of success that elevated everybody in that community. As a result, I and many others walked in a revelation of royalty that manifested as a living reality all around us.

LIFE WITHOUT BOUNDARIES

Like the rest of the South at that time, Tuskegee was racially segregated, but unlike in any other city I knew of, both the Black and White communities in Tuskegee enjoyed high levels of excellence in all areas of life. Each community kept to itself—we had our own Black haberdashery (hatmaker), shopping centers, schools, and so on—but there was no sense of inferiority attached to this separation. Nobody on our side of town was pushing to be like the White establishment downtown, because our community operated at such a high level.

So while Tuskegee had a racial divide, it was almost free of professional and academic restrictions that kept Blacks down, as happened in many other areas of the United States. Black or White, you grew up in Tuskegee believing anything was possible for you. Even during times of civil unrest in other parts of the country, very few protests took place in our city because the Black community didn't feel we lacked anything. Other than not having equal voting rights, Black achievement kept us from feeling educationally and economically deprived. We were living in what was basically a community-wide revelation of royalty.

The fifth-largest Veterans Administration hospital was in town, and many of our fathers and mothers worked there. My own father became a medical technologist and was on call for the hospital. My brother and I went with him many times, and he would instruct me, "William, mix up a 2 percent saline solution." He liked to drill us on these things and prepare us for professional environments. That's why later I became a premed student at college—medicine was what I saw all around me. My mother was an executive secretary at the same VA hospital. My brother designed operating rooms for the VA hospital. My dad also taught science and biology at the college for a while. My sister went to computer school and worked at IBM for thirty years.

Our town was full of Black doctors, professors, and airmen. When I had appendicitis, I was cared for by a nationally prominent Black physician. One local doctor let us scrub down and come into the operating room with him to observe him resetting a bone. My friends' parents were mostly professionals. My brother would go after school to be mentored by the dean of the architecture and engineering department at the local university. He began drafting architectural plans as a high school student and went on to get his master's degree in the subject. Many Black men and women in town started their own businesses. I remember one man who opened the first Black-owned Cadillac dealership in the nation. I thought this was a normal Black community. From heaven's point of view, I believe it was.

As a boy I attended the Chambliss Children's House, where I learned French in the third grade. Our swim meets were held at the University of Alabama, and major music artists like James Brown stopped in town to perform. Future superstar Lionel Richie was born in the same place I was, and for a while he aspired to be like my music group! Nearly every classmate of mine from grade school went away to prep schools in places like New Hampshire. To us, there were no barriers to achievement. Nobody was "less than." Other parts of the country struggled with integration, but in Tuskegee we had everything we wanted. We saw no limitations.

BOOKER T. WASHINGTON'S REVELATION OF ROYALTY

The greatness of Tuskegee, in my view, started with Booker T. Washington, who in 1881 became head of a new institute designed to help formerly enslaved people receive an education. That vision had not existed in Tuskegee before then. It was inside of Washington's heart, and by faith he spoke and manifested it into reality. It really was a work of the kingdom and must have been given to him by God. After receiving a college education in Hampton, Virginia, he came to Tuskegee to build this vision. By the time of Washington's death in 1915, his school had one hundred buildings, fifteen hundred students, two hundred professors and teachers, and financial support from people all over the country. He led an amazing revival of the revelation of royalty, if I can call it that.

One of the pillars of Washington's worldview was that God's goal is not simply to take people to heaven but to establish His kingdom on earth. At that time, ex-slaves and their children had a mindset you find reflected in many slave songs—it was all about crossing over Jordan, leaving this earth and going to heaven to escape suffering. Washington instead believed that God wanted the Black community, and every community, to catch a vision from heaven about how things should be here and now. That was the basis of Washington's teaching.

I have studied Washington's life extensively and admire how he carried himself with the image and personality of a king. When kings are present, others are elevated to greater heights. Washington's students naturally started projects and businesses that made money. They grew cotton, vegetables, and lumber to sell. He taught them trades such as construction and other skills to equip them to create work wherever they went after they graduated. Those he taught and mentored became productive people; some became millionaires. Washington's vision even attracted an experimental program called the Tuskegee Airmen at a time when people thought Blacks couldn't serve as pilots because they didn't have the intelligence. In other words, his vision was catching; it imparted faith to others to do things they previously thought impossible.

Booker T. Washington was an innovator of excellence, operating in the wisdom of God. Proverbs 8 tells us that by wisdom kings rule (v. 15). Washington was a living example of that, and his legacy defined the community long after he was gone.

THINKING BIG

I credit Washington with creating a place where I could be a dreamer. Because of him, I knew it was OK to think big. As a boy, I literally thought I was Superman. If the superhero I saw on television could fly, of course I could fly too. So one day I wrapped a bedsheet around my shoulders and jumped off the garage, thinking I could fly down to my friend Wendell's house. I was that convinced I was invincible. I didn't get hurt too badly, but even my failure to fly that day did not shake my belief that I was Superman.

In my heart of hearts I actually felt I wasn't from Tuskegee. I felt different from my brothers and sisters and everybody else I knew. I saw things bigger. I thought my parents weren't my real parents, and as with Superman, I thought maybe they acquired me through some supernatural means. When people asked me where I was from, I never said Tuskegee, because it was too small for my mind. I always said I was from New York City! I was thinking royally even at a young age. I saw myself in the God class, worthy of living in the biggest, most influential cities. This is how a king thinks—wanting the biggest and the best!

SINGING AND TOURING

Later when I was in college, I needed to make money to support myself, so I started a traveling music group. This was no ordinary group. We had a saxophone, guitar, drums, keyboards, bass, and male and female singers. The guys wore three-piece pinstriped suits, and we toured the East Coast, from New York City down to Florida. We wanted to demonstrate that college students from an out-of-the-way city in Alabama could set the standard of excellence—and, boy, did we.

We rose quickly in popularity and opened for some of the top acts of the day, people whose records still sell and whose songs hit the top of the charts. We played at some of the hottest venues in cities like New York and

Atlanta. Our guitarist was recruited to sit in with one of the biggest acts in pop music when their guitarist was ill. That meant our talent level was high enough to qualify us for top-level gigs.

And yes, I sang and played the keyboard in addition to leading the band on the business side. I always felt there was nothing I couldn't do.

Our group toured for a couple of years before we took different directions in our careers. It was a great experience and typical of what happened in that Tuskegee environment. Nobody told us to be accustomed to mediocrity, so we brought excellence everywhere we went.

VISION TO BECOME A PILOT

Tuskegee also gave me vision to soar higher—quite literally.

My third-grade sweetheart was named Denise, and her father, Daniel "Chappie" James, was one of the most well-known fighter pilots with the Tuskegee Airmen. He had superior flying skills and went on to become the first African American four-star general in the United States Armed Forces. When he wasn't overseas, he sometimes came to our school in uniform to pick up Denise. I saw that uniform and told myself, "I'm going to be like him when I grow up."

Sure enough, when I went to college, I initially thought I was going into medicine, but then I had a strong desire to become a fighter pilot. The image planted in me as a seed when I was very young began to take root. Denise's father never sat down with me and said, "William, would you like to fly someday?" He didn't have to say anything; his influence did all the work.

Here's my point: The revelation of royalty is catching even at a distance. I never knew Booker T. Washington and didn't really speak to Denise's father, but their revelations of excellence and greatness became my own. In the same way, your revelation permeates the environment wherever you go. It is the manifestation of the internal vision into the external atmosphere—and it is powerful.

When I enrolled at Tuskegee University, I joined ROTC, which prepares you for military service. Then I took a test for pilot training, passed, and went to Randolph Air Force Base in San Antonio, Texas. The base was considered the Cadillac of military bases because it was home to the best facilities and the most generals. It was a top-notch, first-class place to be. After training there, I flew fighters—F-4s called Phantoms—for six years and was a flight leader and then an aircraft commander. I received a number of air medals and the Distinguished Flying Cross for my service to our country.

Had I grown up anywhere but Tuskegee, I'm not sure what my life would look like. My community affirmed my desire to be great—to go higher and to learn to rule.

THE DESIRE TO RULE

My father got a taste for royalty at a rich man's home with his aunt, who worked there as a maid. Dad's mother and father had died in Missouri when he was young, so his aunt took him in and raised him in Atlanta. She worked as a maid for the man who owned the *Atlanta Constitution*, one of the biggest newspapers in the South at that time. While she cleaned house, my dad was allowed to sit in with the rich man's son while he was tutored. In a way, my dad was raised part-time in the home of one of the most influential, wealthiest men in the South.

That vision shaped how my dad parented his children. He taught my brother classical violin and made all of us become musicians. He went into the medical industry and had ambitions to own a hotel one day. All of his activities and attitudes fueled my innate desire to rule. I saw in him a sense of greatness.

Some people don't experience royalty in their upbringing like I did, but even those who did must develop this desire. We each have a responsibility to develop a royal mindset. Indeed, when we start thinking royally and seeing above the line, we are simply acting like who we are. Our spirits leap within us, and our hearts connect with it quickly. Royalty makes sense of our lives. We say, "Oh! That's why I think this way and act that way." Your inner royalty wants to manifest in a broken world to make it glorious and whole.

This is why we must continually connect with our desire to rule.

THE SAUDI PRINCE

Not long ago I was traveling to Los Angeles for a speaking engagement when the air traffic control tower told our flight to slow down and circle because the Saudi prince was passing through. The prince was there for a minor medical treatment. I got curious about this man, and when we landed, I noticed that many limousines were pulling away from the airport.

"How many limousines did that prince have?" I asked someone who seemed in the know.

"One hundred," he said.

"What kind of airplanes did he fly in on?" I asked.

"Three 747s and one 777, all for his entourage," he said.

"Where does he stay when he's here?" I wondered aloud.

"He bought out a hotel," the man said.

I later learned that the prince gave everyone on the floor of the medical center he visited a week's trip to Dubai! Everything I observed about the way he traveled provoked me to desire. It was so royal, so generous, so elevating for all involved. Again, it was the biggest and the best. "Why can't God's people be like that?" I thought.

His example of royalty drew on the royal son inside of me.

On a smaller scale, I remember seeing my first Corvette in Montgomery, Alabama, when I was a teenager. That beautiful coupe was sitting on a car lot when I happened to pass by. Wow! Something jumped inside of me when I saw that sporty little car. I couldn't wait to own one. Up to that point I didn't have much money. I was attending college on a partial tennis scholarship, but the music group was starting. One of my motivations with that group was to make enough money to buy that Corvette—and that's exactly what I did. As soon as I made enough money touring, I went down to Montgomery and got that two-door sports car with the removable top. As the saying goes, I was the "tall hog at the trough," let me tell you.

Just as I was drawn to that car, God is drawn to our desire. You read that right—God is attracted to your desires. Isaiah 44:3 says God pours water on ground that is thirsty. This means God is drawn to satisfy our godly desires. He searches for the fire of desire in our hearts, and then He brings answers to fill up those desires. It gives Him pleasure to do this. In fact one of the jobs of the Holy Spirit is to tutor God's children, you and me, into royalty.

God is actually unmoved when we have no desire. What good is water to someone who has no thirst? What good is food when someone has no hunger? It may fill him or her up in a passionless way, but it brings no pleasure to the heart of God. We have to want what God wants to receive God's greatest fulfillment. When we desire to walk royally, God leads us in royalty. It gives Him joy to do this.

The Saudi prince's entourage and mode of living created a desire in me. God is always doing this to each of us—putting something before our eyes to provoke desire that He then fulfills. In Numbers 13, the twelve Hebrew spies brought back the fruit of the Promised Land for inspection by the whole nation. The grape bunches were so enormous that they had to be carried by two men using a pole! But this was not a show-and-tell moment—it was a taste-and-see moment intended to ignite the fire of desire in the people to go up boldly and take the Promised Land. But the people didn't connect to their desire for that fruit. They talked instead about the obstacles—the giants, the walls—until they clung to the obstacles and forgot about the opportunity. Their hearts desired to believe the bad report, and so God fulfilled that desire. They wandered and died in the desert until the next generation went in to possess the land.

Desire draws out answers from God. But we must set our desires on godly things. This is why Psalm 34:8 says, "O taste and see that the LORD is good."

AMBASSADORS

During my first missionary trip to Haiti, the poverty I saw was astounding. But in the middle of the capital city was a huge white building surrounded by well-kept grounds. People were lined up to get into the place every day.

"What is that place?" I asked my host.

"The American embassy," he replied. "Those people are lined up to try to get permission to come to the United States."

"Does somebody live there too?" I asked.

"The ambassador," my host said.

Some might be offended that an ambassador should live in such a nice place when surrounded by such misery, but to me it was a valuable lesson and my first revelation of how the kingdom of God works in the earth. You were never made to live at the level of the country God sent you to but at the level of the country you were sent from. That's why the Saudi prince's entourage struck me not as ostentatious but as heavenly. As they say, "game knows game." Kings and queens should be drawn to royal examples around them.

KINGS OWN EVERYTHING

One time I was going to meet a governor of one of the states in Nigeria. At that time I had a little handheld video player, which I was going to use to show him some things happening in the US. Before we met this man in his court, a fellow minister I was traveling with said, "You're not going to take that in there, are you?"

"Yes, why?" I responded.

"If you do, and he asks for it, you have to give it to him," my friend warned.

Again, someone might be offended by that, but I was impressed! Here was a man who saw himself as an owner, not a beggar or borrower. He was acting like a king! Kings rule by decree, and lords function by ownership. That's why God is the King of kings and Lord of lords. He owns everything—even you and me. "The earth is the LORD'S, and the fulness thereof; the world, and they that dwell therein" (Ps. 24:1). This man had the same mindset, that whatever was brought into his court was under his jurisdiction. He was a man who understood authority.

Kings who act like beggars are called evil in the Bible. Ecclesiastes 10:5–7 tells us there is an evil under the sun when a king leads a horse while the unrighteous sits in the saddle. God calls living beneath your level of authority evil. It's a trick of the enemy to try to get kings and queens to act like beggars, borrowers, and servants.

Look at the story of Lazarus in Luke chapter 16. This story, told by Jesus, gets preached all sorts of ways, but I'd like you to see it in terms of a man living beneath his royalty. Lazarus, a beggar, lived right outside a rich man's gate. He had sores on his body, could barely move, and spent his days crying out for provision. But when Lazarus died, he went into Abraham's bosom—that is, paradise. Lazarus was a king, but he didn't know it until then. On earth he allowed himself to act like and be treated like a beggar. But a beggar was never who he was. This is the reality of far too many children of God. They act the part of the beggar when God has called them to be kings or queens.

T. L. Osborn once shared about a painter working on a canvas when a beggar spied him from across the street and asked, "Why are you looking at me?"

The painter said, "I'm painting a portrait of you. In fact, I just finished."

"Can I see it?" the beggar requested, and the painter welcomed him to look. On the canvas the beggar saw a man smartly dressed in a suit, carrying a briefcase and striding confidently down the sidewalk.

"Is that me?" the beggar asked.

"Yes, that's the you that I see," the painter said.

Something transformed in the beggar's heart in that moment, and he said, "Then that's the me I will be." He left the spot where he begged and went on to live a different, more successful life.

In the same way, God, through the ministry of the Holy Spirit, is constantly tutoring us to walk in the fullness of our royalty.

Possessing Your Inheritance

God wants to distinguish you through superior performance and royal character so that those around you will want to know your God and follow you as their leader. That's called influence. He will give you answers to seemingly impossible problems that no one else can solve. He will give you a vision of your greatness—Tuskegee vision—and a revelation of royalty that enlarges your influence on the earth.

In the Old Testament there was a man named Jabez who sought the Lord to change his life and destiny. *Jabez* literally means "sorrow" or "he causes pains."[1] This tells us something very important: though Jabez started out in a life full of hardship, struggle, and low self-image, he somehow received a revelation of his royalty such that he could make this noble request of God:

> Jabez cried to the God of Israel, saying, Oh, that You would bless me and enlarge my border, and that Your hand might be with me, and You would keep me from evil so it might not hurt me! And God granted his request.
>
> —1 CHRONICLES 4:10, AMPC

As a result, God considered Jabez "more honourable than his brethren" (1 Chron. 4:9). Think of that! When Jabez escaped the story of his pain and embraced his story as a king, God enlarged his influence and his wallet *and* considered him more honorable than his brethren! That amazing result is available to you and me. When Jabez behaved like a son of the King, God related to him as such.

What does the Lord have for you to do on the earth? How can He enlarge your capacity to receive your royal inheritance, to accomplish great things for the kingdom?

Ask God to open your eyes—your spiritual sight—to see who you are. Ask Him to bring before your eyes examples of royalty such as I had in Tuskegee and like the Saudi prince, the ambassador to Haiti, and my own father. Think big! Pray big, like Jabez did, and allow God to tutor you into His vision for you as a royal child and a righteous ruler on the earth.

CHAPTER 6

MY KINGDOM BUSINESS ASSIGNMENT

❖―――――――――――――❖

O
NE OF THE major ways God tutored me in royalty was by having me work at IBM for fourteen
years in increasing levels of leadership. He gave
me this experience not for my own good—as I thought
at the time—but for the good of many others whom I
would later lead and teach. Before I was even born again,
He was giving me revelations about royalty that I would
later share with others.

I finished serving as a fighter pilot and was honorably
discharged from the United States Air Force. At that
point I decided to go into the business world. I was an
arrogant fighter pilot who didn't know the Lord but who
had every confidence in my own abilities. I felt there
was nothing I couldn't do, so when I heard IBM was in
a hiring freeze, it didn't bother me one bit. I knew my
image would speak for itself and they would hire me. I
was so confident that while taking a tour of a branch
office I saw a sales leader board and read the name at
the top.

"Who's that?" I asked, indicating the name.

"That's our top sales leader," my host said.

"You can consider him beat," I responded. I was that confident, but of course a lot of human pride was in there as well. God needed to work that out of me so I'd have a pure revelation of royalty undiluted by bravado. Still, my sense of royalty had me convinced that there was no hurdle too high for me to jump over.

BUM ASSIGNMENT?

IBM hired me and assigned me to sell computers to the medical industry in a certain geographical area. I was very pleased, but after I attended training, they changed my assignment to nonprofits. This seemed like a disaster, and I went home fuming.

"This is not going to work!" I said to myself. "There's no money and no sales in that territory. What would motivate a nonprofit to buy millions of dollars of computers?"

Then I fell through each rung of blame on the tall ladder of bitterness.

"They're prejudiced against me! They're threatened by what I can do. They're trying to keep me down and protect others." On and on I went. Then I schemed my escape, figuring that this bum assignment was merely training to go somewhere else. Maybe I wasn't supposed to work long-term for IBM but get my foot in the door of the industry and then take those skills elsewhere.

Finally, I came to a settled place, put all the blame aside, and saw the situation for what it was: an assignment I didn't want but an assignment nonetheless. Turning it down wouldn't solve anything. "If I can fly fighters, I can try to make this work," I concluded and decided to give it a shot. Swallowing my pride as best I could, I polished up my business presentation and began meeting with large and smaller nonprofit leaders in the downtown Chicago territory I was assigned.

Guess what? It turned out just as I thought. Those people wouldn't buy a thing. My negative predictions all came true. Of course, I blindly blamed IBM, the nonprofit leaders, my managers, my coworkers, and anybody else in sight. Remember, I wasn't born again yet!

Then one night, Debbie, a coworker in the sales department, saw me working late and said, "Winston, come, let's have coffee." She sat me down and laid out some advice.

"Your problem is that you come across like you know everything. Your presentation is too perfect. You leave no room," she said.

I had tried to make everything perfect. That was my fighter pilot training, absolute precision.

"If you're perfect, customers feel they have no room to make a decision, no options. It's all locked in, and they don't like that," she said. "When you're making your presentation, misspell a word or something. Give them some room to be right."

That seemed like crazy advice, but I was willing to try anything. The next day at a presentation I intentionally fumbled a word here and there, and I misspelled a word on the written materials. To my amazement, it worked! I made the sale. Oh, happy day! That client signed on the bottom line and bought that computer. I was so happy about it I almost didn't know what to do. My appearance of perfection and superiority had been a barrier to my business success, a barrier to relationships, and so on. To grow and mature, I had to humble myself. Now I could see that IBM was teaching me some things.

I put that lesson to work from then on and got to be the top salesman in our office in new accounts. My customers were not IBM customers. They may have never purchased an IBM computer, so I had to bring them over to our side and convince them to try a new brand of computer system. It wasn't easy, and it took a lot of knowledge and some performance, but mostly it took eating humble pie wherever I went. I approached these meetings saying, "Let me be your partner, not your adversary. I am not here to push something on you that you don't want or need. My goal is for your organization to become more efficient and your people to be more pleased with you than ever before. I think this could help you."

That change of approach made a world of difference. It still amazes me how one little click of the key will open a new door. They saw the true value in what I was selling.

SEASON SHIFT

I did so well with that territory that they gave me additional industry opportunities, banking and manufacturing too. I made more money that year than I had ever imagined. I was now a shooting star at IBM, rising through the sales ranks. I had favor with the upper leadership and with my peers. For instance, the company was always training its employees, and when we traveled to New York or elsewhere to receive training, the trainers had each group select a few representatives. I was chosen by my fellow employees to be president of three training classes and vice president of another. These fellow students were from Ivy League universities and such. They didn't know me, but after a few days together they selected me. I believe now that they heard confidence or royalty in my voice that even I didn't know was there.

The most important thing to happen to me at IBM was that I was born again. It happened in my first couple of years, when I was struggling. Everything seemed to be falling apart, and I cried out to God for help. A secretary invited me to what I found out was a church meeting, and that night I gave my life to the Lord. I later met Veronica at IBM, and we were married. Life was going very well, and God blessed us abundantly.

Due to a nice promotion, we moved from Chicago to Minneapolis. From a business point of view, I thrived in Minnesota. We were given the task of selling computers to some of the largest companies, such as 3M. I had reached a kind of pinnacle and was even setting my sights on possibly becoming a president of one of the divisions at IBM.

But the winds were changing for me, and little things began to demonstrate it. One day when I was leading a company branch meeting with seven or eight managers, a marketing manager commented out of the blue, "You know, Bill, sometimes you sound like a preacher." For some reason, that statement embarrassed me and I snapped at him, "Why don't you mind your own business and sell something so everyone at this branch will be happy?" He took it as a joke, but I really felt indignant about the comment he had made. It reminded me of the time a lady at church had told me, "You know, you're going to be a preacher." I thanked her and never spoke to her again! That's how much I did not want to hear those words. Yet those people saw something in me that I could not hide—a calling bigger than selling computer systems and climbing corporate ladders.

By that time in my Christian walk I was avidly listening to every teaching on the kingdom of God and faith I could get my hands on. I didn't care if the preacher was Baptist, Pentecostal, or of some other stripe. I was hungry to study faith and wanted to hear about it from anyone who really believed and operated in it. God was drawing me to the message I would one day preach, but all I knew then was I was hungry to learn.

At work I was doing well, but things weren't clicking along like they had before. Work felt more like drudgery. The wind was no longer at my back. I wasn't enjoying it as much as I used to. Worse yet, those irritating comments stuck in my mind, and I had to acknowledge the truth in them. I did feel that something was pulling me away from IBM. I wasn't sure what it was, but I knew I had a desire for the things of God—to preach, as those people had said.

"What is happening here?" I wondered. Up to then I never wanted to be a preacher. Preachers didn't have the clout, success, or money I dreamed of having. They didn't own big houses like company presidents own. These thoughts ran circles in my mind until finally Veronica and I decided to take a little step of faith by starting a weekly Bible study in our apartment in Edina, a suburb of Minneapolis.

Before we knew it, that little study began to grow. One night the Lord really tested me. A woman piped up right in the middle of the meeting and said, "What keeps me from being baptized right now?" I had been teaching from Acts 8, where the Ethiopian eunuch asks that same question in verse 36: "And as they went on their way, they came unto a certain water: and the eunuch said, See, here is water; what doth hinder me to be baptized?"

I said quickly, "Water. We're in an apartment."

"This apartment complex has a pool downstairs," she said.

"Well, there might be people in it," I said lamely. I was trying to figure out how to tell her no! Of course, I had started it by teaching about a man being baptized on the side of a road!

"Those people can move aside!" this woman declared. "I brought my bathing suit. I'm ready to be baptized."

She wasn't kidding—she had actually brought her bathing suit! "There's no way I can tell her no," I thought. I felt truly convicted by her faith—and my own embarrassment—as I led her and the others down to the apartment swimming pool. In truth, I was cringing as fourteen of us gathered around a shallow corner of the pool. I felt the eyes of my neighbors burning into me as our group watched the excited woman. Eager to get it over with, I baptized her, and the people applauded. The ones not with our group stared at us wondering, "What is that man doing?"

That was my first baptism—not pretty on my end, but

at least I accepted the challenge. That woman remained on fire for the Lord and developed into a powerful, wonderful servant of His kingdom. It's amazing what God can do.

Yet while my sense of decorum was violated, that baptism gave me and Veronica a breakthrough in our thinking about what God could do with us. We sensed more was to come—and not all of it was going to be comfortable.

YMCA CHURCH

I was traveling the Midwest for IBM, but meanwhile our Bible study had outgrown our apartment, so we rented a room at the local YMCA on Sunday mornings for meetings. Soon there were too many to fit in that room, so we moved to a bigger room in a different YMCA. Pretty soon our meetings looked like church meetings, with times of worship, teaching, and testimony. Some people volunteered to play and sing for the praise times, while others stood at the door and greeted people. By the Spirit, people stepped into various roles. We hardly had to organize it. God was clearly giving shape to what was happening. Veronica and I marveled at what was happening.

At that time I thought in terms of having two careers, one at IBM and a part-time one in ministry, because that's what my life looked like. The problem was that I couldn't find any examples of someone doing that. I was making it up as I went. Then the two worlds began to intermingle. One day at IBM a woman who worked for me said, "I heard you've got a little church." I had been keeping my church a secret as best as I could, but I told her she was right; I did.

"Where is it?" she asked. "I might drive down there sometime."

I told her, and sure enough, she attended a meeting soon after that. On that morning, after our praise and worship time I got up, greeted everyone, and told the story of how I got born again. I noticed a hand in the back go up. It was the woman who worked for me.

"Yes?" I said, calling her by name.

"I want to be saved," she said simply.

"You what?" I responded.

"I want to be saved," she repeated.

I said the most ridiculous thing you could say in that circumstance: "Wait until the end of service when we call people forward." Her hand went down, and I said a few more words. Suddenly her hand went up again.

"Yes?" I said patiently.

"I want to be saved right now," she said. People burst out laughing and clapping. I knew she was in the right, even though in my immature ministry mind we were interrupting the normal flow of things.

"All right, come on up," I said. "Anybody else want to be saved?"

Six or seven other people came up! I then realized that simply telling the story of my testimony had inspired them. It gave them a vision for new life in Christ and was the seed that drew out their desire to be saved. What I had said was uncomplicated but bore instant fruit.

That was how God worked with me then. Every time He moved me forward, I went from comfort to discomfort in the unknown. Every time I wondered, "How am I going to operate in this new place?" He was faithful to teach me, and so I grew in ministry step-by-step.

Soon other IBM employees came to the church and were born again as well. We outgrew that bigger room and desired our own building where we could come pray anytime. We found a place for lease in a needy part of town, named ourselves Mission Temple of Faith, and the ministry continued to grow.

LEAVING IBM

I share this next part to show you how messy and uncertain it can feel when walking in the will of God. For me, at least, it was not a straight line flooded with light and certainty. Far from it!

At that time a certain Bible passage stuck in my heart like a burr. It came from a message I heard someone preach about seedtime and harvest. In Mark 10:29–30 Jesus says, "There is no man that hath left house, or brethren, or sisters, or father, or mother, or wife, or children, or lands, for my sake, and the gospel's, but he shall receive an hundredfold now in this time, houses, and brethren, and sisters, and mothers, and children, and lands, with persecutions; and in the world to come eternal life."

I began to meditate on those words. They echoed inside of me: "Receive an hundredfold *now* in this time." My meditation on that passage not only transformed my mind but gave me a glimpse of my future that pulled me in the direction of my destiny. In my own comfortable way of thinking, I didn't like the idea of leaving the business world and entering full-time ministry—but I did like the idea of receiving a hundredfold of what I had at the time. God uses tastes of your glorious future to get you where He wants you to go. Through biblical meditation, I no longer saw myself going into poverty by going into full-time ministry. I saw a glorious future.

But it seemed as if as soon as I latched on to those words by faith, all kinds of forces came against me, especially in the area of our finances. At the time, we had only one income. Veronica had just had David and did not return to work after maternity leave. We had the expenses of a new baby, our house needed repairs, and we had other expenses. "How will I ever pay for these things without my job at IBM?" I wondered again and again. That's when the words of Jesus held me firm and made me unshakable. "No one who leaves anything for the sake of the gospel will fail to receive a hundredfold—now!"

Soon the light of revelation broke forth in me, and I knew God was confirming His will for me to leave IBM. Whenever light comes, struggles cease. It happened while I was driving down the road in Minnesota. The next thing I knew, I had pulled over to the side of the road and called Veronica.

"Baby, I am leaving this company," I told her confidently.

"Well, praise the Lord!" she said, as if she'd been waiting for me to settle on it.

With Jesus' words clearly in mind, I walked into my boss' office one day. Clarity makes you daring. I knew I was leaving a good thing for something better.

"I am leaving IBM today," I announced without a

waver in my voice. He looked at me like I had lost my ever-loving mind.

"Are you going somewhere else?" he asked, thinking he was losing me to the competition. That would have been a strike against him, to lose someone he had trained.

"No," I said and assured him that my future plans were no longer in the computer industry. He still couldn't believe it.

"Take two weeks off," he said. "Don't think about the company. We'll take care of everything."

I did that, and in an effort to keep me, IBM proposed that I stay in Minnesota and be the company's advocate with the public. They offered to pay me the same salary. To be honest, that sounded great, and so I went home, spent the early morning in prayer, and offered their proposal to God. He pretty well thundered a response from Genesis 14 in my heart: "Let no man say he has made Abraham rich." (See verse 23.) Wow! He was not kidding around, and I had no choice but to obey. I went into work after the two weeks were up.

"So what do you think?" my boss asked.

"I think that not only am I leaving, I'm leaving right away," I told him. He and others must have thought religion had addled my brain, but all I cared about was being obedient to the word of the Lord. The situation was only becoming clearer to me.

Not long after that, a branch manager in Milwaukee called me. This man was a lapsed Catholic with a drinking problem and a rough life. But the story he shared with me was amazing.

"Bill, what happened to you?" he asked with great

concern in his voice. "I'm not a religious man, but I was driving and I saw your face in the clouds. What happened to you?"

I fairly rejoiced at this strange confirmation.

"I am going into the ministry," I told him boldly. "Thank God, I made the right decision."

The morning after I left IBM for good, Veronica came into my study and said, "Sweetheart, God spoke to me about you going to seminary." She didn't know that He had spoken the same thing to me! All I could say was, "Wow." I knew something was happening beyond what either of us could imagine. A few days later we put our house on the market. It sold in one day.

We had always prayed, "God, let us be on the front lines and leading edge of what You're doing." He was taking us up on our request.

Interestingly, all the people at IBM who thought I was crazy and even shunned me for a period of time came back to me over the years and reestablished relationships. One manager got saved in part because of my exit. Another woman who admitted she previously thought I'd lost my mind came to me years later wanting to enroll in our church's business school! What an amazing thing.

I had left the corporate world and was about to receive a whole other kind of training—starting at the bottom, not the top.

CHAPTER 7

CHICAGO BEGINNINGS

⟶ ⟵

WHEN I LEFT IBM, my wife and I immediately moved to Tulsa, Oklahoma, where I attended seminary and Veronica declared and received that job working in computers. After a relatively short season there, we felt God's call to move back to Chicago to pursue our kingdom destiny there.

People often speak of small beginnings, but our return to Chicago was truly small and humbling. Veronica and I returned to Chicago with our young son, David, and only $200. We had no place to stay, and a dear sister in Christ, Sister Beverly, opened her home to us and took care of us until we could get established. We lived with Sister Beverly for almost eight months.

One Saturday, after a meeting that we were holding at the Quality Inn on Halsted Street, a minister who was in the audience asked if I would speak to her church group that met in a small storefront building on the corner of Lake Street and Pulaski Road on Chicago's West Side. I accepted and went there to speak a short time later.

After I finished speaking, God directed me to lay

hands on the sick and cast out devils. As I did, miracles broke out! The minister who invited me said, "God is telling me to turn this place over to you right now!" It happened so quickly, I said, "Whoa, wait a minute. Hold on now. Let me go and pray about this." When I went back to Sister Beverly's house and prayed, God said, "Take it," and I did. That was the start of our first church in Chicago.

ANOINTING THE STREETS

We named the church Living Word Church of Chicago, and it was located in one of the highest-crime districts in the Windy City. Most of the people there had no money. I was pretty sure they didn't even have bank accounts. The neighborhood was really rough on the eyes—buildings were old and run-down. Next to the "church" building was a place where people frequently gambled. The owner of our building didn't take checks to pay the rent, only cash.

Here's how bad it was: my wife's family members, who are from Chicago, wouldn't even come to our services.

One day when a few of us were praying before service, an older woman who lived in the neighborhood came to the church. She said, "I need to speak with the pastor."

I said, "I'm the pastor. How can I help you?"

She explained that drug dealers had taken over her block and were refusing to leave, and now all the residents were afraid to go outside. The children couldn't even go out to play. I told her to join the prayer circle, and we prayed right then. I didn't know what God was going to say or do, but I listened for His instructions.

He told me, "Take a bottle of anointing oil, bless it, and tell the woman to pour it down the middle of her street."

"Well, give it here!" the woman said, and I handed her the bottle of anointing oil I happened to be carrying. Then she left.

A few days later she came back and testified that she did exactly as I instructed. She said the drug dealers came back the next day, stayed for about an hour, then packed up and never returned. No police were involved. God's solution had worked overnight! Praise God!

I only wish every problem in the neighborhood had disappeared with them. We still had to sweep broken liquor bottles away from our building's front entrance before services. Then one evening while we were in service, someone stole our car. I was literally teaching on demons and deliverance when one of those demons came around and stole my car!

Now my family had no transportation, so we took the L train from our apartment to the church, with Veronica often holding our son with one hand and her guitar in her other hand. After going through a freezing Chicago winter, we eventually got another car. The church was at this location for almost one year, and although we experienced hardship, not once did we fear going there. We knew and confessed that the Lord was our protector, shield, and strength, and we moved forward in faith. We were never harmed.

SEEING TEN THOUSAND

While we were at Lake and Pulaski, we had no visible, natural proof that our ministry efforts would work. We did it all by faith, with no one backing us and no other church supporting us. We were living above the line, where provision flows directly from God, our provider. It was by pure faith that I knew the ministry would grow. Back when I was in seminary, I could see in my mind's eye ten thousand people attending our future church, so low numbers didn't bother me at all. I knew we'd get there. While living in Tulsa, we were members of a large church whose Sunday services were held in a huge sports arena of a local university. God made sure to keep a big vision before us, even in leaner times. Like Joseph in the Book of Genesis, I could see the future before it actualized. When you keep the vision before you, it makes you daring, persistent, and courageous. It keeps you excited. I knew my purpose was beginning to manifest despite our humble beginnings. God was going to do much more.

Meanwhile, we remained faithful. Veronica played the guitar while I led praise and worship. The tiny room fit about forty people. The Word was going out, and God drew people to His vision, His mission, and His message. One member drove about thirty miles twice a week from Gary, Indiana, to attend services. In my mind we were seeing a small fulfillment of Ezekiel 36, which talks about the Lord rebuilding the waste places. I knew that one day people would pass by our church and say, "Wow, look at that. It used to be a wasteland, but now it looks like Eden." It was a prophetic location, not a pathetic one.

One memory of our time at Lake and Pulaski is seared

into my mind. During a particular service, I walked up and down the narrow aisles between folding chairs when the Spirit of God came upon me and I shouted, "You must see yourself as royalty!" The words came straight from the Spirit. To the natural mind the declaration probably sounded foolish. Our church could hardly have been poorer. Many of our members were school dropouts, some couldn't read and were very needy, but they loved God. When I spoke those words, I wasn't speaking from what I saw with my natural eyes. I was speaking what God had shown me as part of His plan for their lives and for our ministry.

PRAYING WITH POWER

I was learning things in the trenches of ministry that I couldn't learn in cockpits or corporate meeting rooms. We almost had to get down to nothing to understand God's ability to care for us so that we could care for others. Truth be told, I wasn't seasoned enough to pastor a larger group at that time. I would have made too many mistakes, so God started us small. He was training us for royalty, for rulership, for reigning, and I needed new humility to make me teachable so God could give me proper influence over others. Pride came easily when flying jets and managing people at a big company. God was shaping my heart in new ways, and He chose that environment to do it in. I never felt punished or pushed aside. I knew great things lay ahead.

A few months after starting the church, Veronica and I had moved out of Sister Beverly's house into an efficiency, or studio, apartment, then into a two-bedroom place. Getting that efficiency apartment was a miracle in itself. We had no money for the security deposit and no furniture, but the Lord granted us favor with the management office. They even let us use furniture from the model apartment until we were able to purchase some of our own.

To pray early in the morning without disturbing the family, I would walk to the high school football stadium across the street from our apartment. In the quiet hours of the new day I would walk around the track praying, then sit on the bleachers and read my Bible. I did that for months, but I was doing more than walking and reading. I was decreeing the Scriptures and legislating my future.

You see, though we were in a rough environment at the church, the rough environment wasn't in us. When I prayed, I rehearsed who I was—my royalty, my divine commission, and my character. Joshua 1:3 tells us, "Every place that the sole of your foot will tread upon I have given to you, just as I promised to Moses" (ESV). With every step I took, I was proclaiming my jurisdiction over that area, my destiny in life, my royal calling as a son of the King.

Walking around that track, I made faith confessions about my family, our ministry, and our finances. I confessed the truth over and over until I had what some people call a breakthrough, or a sense of being settled in the Spirit. It's like a transaction of the spirit when you feel like you've completed a thing and it has become certain. Whatever you desire in prayer already exists in the spirit, and now you have taken ownership of it by faith. You possess the "title deed." (See Hebrews 11:1, AMPC.)

I had always been a praying man, but I learned afresh how our true power is in prayer. It transports you above the line and into perceiving an accurate image of yourself. It causes you to soar above man's logic to a place of supernatural guidance and provision. I kept praying according to the answer, not the problem. God deals only with answers. Some people come before God and fill the air with their problems. God knows the problems. He never told us to pray about what is wrong in our lives. He told us in Mark 11:24 to pray for our desires and when we pray to believe that we receive the things we desire, and we shall have them. The idea is to keep the answer before you in prayer—because focusing on the answer brings faith.

I learned again and again to respond to every situation with the Word of God. Why? Because God's Word is the all-controlling factor in every situation. When you pray the problem, you establish and embed the wrong things in your heart. You end up thinking about your troubles and talking about them to yourself and others. God does not respond to these types of prayers—but demons sure do.

The world has its psychic hotlines, but did you know there are also psychic prayers? What do I mean? Words that do not line up with God's Word give demons license to try to bring those words to pass. The Bible calls it sorcery, which involves demons enforcing words spoken by someone aligning himself or herself with the kingdom of darkness. The more we meditate on problems caused by the enemy, the more we empower the work of the enemy and magnify his name. May it never be!

God wants hearts focused on answers, not problems, because these flow from the Word of God and the will of God. When we empower the answer with our attention and agreement, it will soon manifest and bring the problem to nothing.

Let me ask you: Does your prayer life line up with the Word of God? If not, what is the substance of your prayers? Are they a laundry list of complaints and wants? If you are praying words that God didn't say or that were not conceived from the Holy Spirit, they will not yield the results you want. God watches over His Word to perform it—He doesn't watch over your word or the enemy's word but *His* Word. Pray things that God can respond to. You don't have to elevate your voice or pray in a certain place or position or for a certain amount of time. The power is in His Word. Say what God says and line up your prayers with His Word. That is how to pray with power and get results.

When you do this, angels literally fight your battles for you. We are not alone in the walk of faith. A great inspiration to me in that season when we were growing our ministry was a book by Cindy Trimm called *Commanding Your Morning*. She encouraged readers to wake up and decree things that angels then help bring to pass throughout the day. I believe firmly in this, and I live this way. It is the culture of a king to have servants. As children of God, our Father sends angels, ministering spirits, to work on our behalf. They set up pathways of productivity and avenues of success. Angels aren't empowered by complaints, problems, or lies. God sends them on assignment only once you've verbalized your agreement with heavenly decrees. This is why God warned Moses in Exodus 23 to watch his mouth.

> Behold, I send an angel before you to guard you on the way and to bring you to the place that I have prepared. Pay careful attention to him and obey his voice; do not rebel against him, for he will not pardon your transgression, for my name is in him. But if you carefully obey his voice and do all that I say, then I will be an enemy to your enemies and an adversary to your adversaries.
>
> —EXODUS 23:20–22, ESV

When you see the promised land ahead of you, and when your words agree with the decrees of the King of kings, then God will move you to the address He has reserved for you—even if it takes a little time.

THE KEYS TO WEALTH

In those early Chicago days, we had no means of financial support aside from the church, and that wasn't much. But we didn't need much. Veronica hadn't had a new dress in four years, but neither of us complained. We faithfully followed the kingdom law of sowing and reaping, and in due season our family moved from the apartment to a brand-new house that was for rent. It was a blessing from God because it gave us more space.

Still, funds were tight. At one point we wanted a keyboard for the church to use for praise and worship, so we went to a large music store chain to buy one. The salesman asked us, "What kind of keyboard would you like?"

"What do you have?" I asked.

"I have this one. It's new, and it's called a KORG," he said.

He started playing the instrument, which sounded like an orchestra.

"How much is it?" I asked.

"A little over $3,000," he replied, and I about choked. You could get a car for that much!

"Well," I said, "you can take me to the ones that cost $150 because that's all I have to spend."

He escorted us to the cheap keyboards, and while we were looking at them, a guy came into the store who belonged to a rock and roll band. He had blue and yellow hair and rings on every finger. I watched as he bought two of those KORGs on the spot!

I thought, "Here we are serving Jesus with all our hearts, and we can't even buy a decent keyboard for the church." I wasn't angry, but it was a reality check for me. I was provoked to believe for more. It wasn't right for worldly musicians to have better instruments than God's children!

This and many other lessons shaped us during those lean Chicago years—but soon God would move us to our new address and raise us up higher, into the realm of the royal vision for ministry He had given to us.

PART III

LEARNING TO RECEIVE

·⊷— AND —⊷·

PROSPER

CHAPTER 8

REAPING YOUR ROYAL INHERITANCE

❖———————————————————❖

T HERE COMES A time when you start reaping the royal inheritance that you have decreed by faith. It's impossible to know when this will happen or how long it will take to get there. Nothing in your preparation or your background will help you figure it out—it simply happens in God's time and in His way. It's always a wonderful thing to behold and participate in. God's timing is perfect.

For example, one man got saved in prison and started listening to my teachings while incarcerated. (This was later in my ministry.) This man began to confess God's Word over his life, family, and finances as I so often exhort people to do. He had only a third-grade education, but he got his PhD in the revelation of royalty. Over and over he listened to my teachings and did what I said to do, and that is how he grew into God's image of himself as a royal son.

After serving his time, this man was released and got a job making $4.50 per hour mowing lawns. Then he got another job making $12 per hour at a manufacturing plant. He continued to legislate his success and eventually showed up one day at our church to share his testimony.

"From listening to Pastor Winston's teaching, I want to let you know I have a new Mercedes, an SUV, and am about to purchase a Rolls-Royce," he said. "I have a seven-bedroom home and four Jacujees."

He couldn't even pronounce *Jacuzzi*, but he owned four of them. Imagine the transformation in this man's life. He went from being a grade-school dropout and criminal to walking in his quite prosperous identity in the household of God. What a story!

If that doesn't encourage you to take the limits off God, maybe nothing will. The revelation of royalty launches us into a whole new realm of possibilities—and line of wealth. God has plans to take you somewhere great. It may be through a problem you can't solve or into a lifestyle you can't presently afford. He is God Almighty. His power and your faith combined can open every door and accomplish every glorious assignment He has for you.

But it has to be on His terms—not through earthly toil but by heavenly revelation.

How We Produce: The Seed Principle

We arrived back in Chicago without announcement to friends and relatives or much fanfare. We arrived with just $200, and the only open door was to Sister Beverly's house. Where we started our ministry (on Chicago's West Side, an economically distressed part of the city) was as unimpressive and unnoticeable (but full of potential) as tiny seeds in a seed packet.

A seed is not flashy. It has no flowers—except invisible

ones inside of it. It has no green foliage—except the ones waiting inside to grow. It has no fruit and really nothing to recommend itself—except for the potential it carries. In the same way, my ministry destiny may not have been apparent to others, but God's revelation of royalty had shown me what was inside of me. I not only had righteousness, peace, and joy in the Holy Ghost, but I had influence waiting to burst forth. I could feel it working before it manifested. It was like that Superman dream from my boyhood; it was all geared up and ready to break forth from me and do great things in the world. Nobody could see it but us and a small group of believers who invited me to speak.

That's the thing about a seed: it may not seem like much, but it possesses the power to grow all on its own. It is self-contained, bearing its own life, and is designed to be sown in the worst environments to turn them into the Garden of Eden. Only God can start with a seed and end up with a forest. This is the nature of the kingdom, as Jesus said.

> Whereunto shall we liken the kingdom of God? or with what comparison shall we compare it? It is like a grain of mustard seed, which, when it is sown in the earth, is less than all the seeds that be in the earth: but when it is sown, it groweth up, and becometh greater than all herbs, and shooteth out great branches; so that the fowls of the air may lodge under the shadow of it.
>
> —MARK 4:30–32

sus said the kingdom of God is not like just any old seed but like a grain of mustard seed. What is special about a mustard seed? It is one of the smallest seeds you can plant. If you drop it on the floor, it is hard to find. Yet it carries enormous potential. As "seeds," we all enter the world small and unimpressive. You can hardly identify who is going to be used before God begins to grow them before your eyes. But once these people come into their place and assignment in the kingdom of God, though they were once the smallest in position, influence, or size, they grow up and become the greatest among all the other seeds (people) planted there. I have seen this work many times, and it is awesome.

Jesus also compared words to seeds. In Chicago, God taught us to sow the Word, according to Mark 4:14, "The sower soweth the word," and Luke 8:11, "The seed is the word of God." He taught us how to use the Word of God to get our needs met. He taught us that ministry requires sowing the Word of the kingdom and financial seed and letting God give the increase. We saw in real life that a seed is the tool God gives us to meet any need. One man of God said it this way: "Sow what you have been given to create something you have been promised." Oh, I like that!

Understand, a seed can be many things: love, patience, time, kindness, money, or anything that is of value to the sower. Peter sowed his boat and later his life (Luke 5:3, 10–11). A young boy sowed his lunch of five loaves and two small fish (Matt. 14:19), and God sowed His only begotten Son, Jesus (John 3:16).

When you sow a seed in faith, whatever it is, your

harvest is guaranteed. (See Galatians 6:7.) I learned this firsthand as a college student before I was even saved when I went to work at, of all things, a tobacco farm.

HAZARDVILLE TRAINING

Summer was coming, and as a young college student, I was eager to have money to spend on things I wanted. I had cut lawns for money before, but it hadn't produced as much income as I hoped. Then I saw an advertisement at college for a job in Connecticut that seemed to offer good work. Another advantage was that I would get away from Alabama during the summer when it is as hot as blazes. I was only too happy to go north during those sweltering months, so I applied for the Connecticut job and was accepted. The advertisement had said the job was "working at a tobacco company." I would soon find out what that meant.

They sent me a bus ticket, and I rode up from Tuskegee. It seemed to take a week! I arrived in the town of Hazardville, where the company was located—the name should have given me fair warning of what was to come. I had pictured myself working in a business or corporate setting, as implied by the word "company." But when I got there, I learned what my duties would be: planting and picking tobacco.

"You mean working in a field?" I asked.

"Yes," said the company representative.

"I thought I was doing something else," I replied.

"Nope," said the representative. "This is what you came to do. And by the way, you can't leave, because you owe us for the bus ticket."

I was trapped! I went into the dorm room where I and other tobacco pickers would sleep and dumped all my toiletries and belongings on one of the bunk beds. I went to the restroom, and when I came back, half my stuff was gone. "You have got to be kidding me," I said under my breath. "This is going to be a long summer."

Hoping to get out of the whole thing, I called my dad that day, but he didn't budge.

"Oh, son, it'll be all right," he advised me. "Give it a few more days."

I think he also didn't want to spring for the bus ticket I would need to get from Hazardville back to Alabama. So I was stuck. Like it or not, I would be a tobacco picker that summer.

Our days started at 4:30 in the morning. We each wore two pairs of pants and took a piece of square cardboard to put on the ground to sit on. Rows of furrowed dirt stretched so far you couldn't see the ends of them. Our job was to plant little tobacco seedlings the length of a man's hand all along those endless rows. Each of us was assigned a row, and we put the cardboard down, plopped on top of it, and began scooting and planting. That's what we did all day long: scoot and plant, thousands of times, down in the dirt from sunup to sundown. I began to miss Alabama, no matter how hot it was!

Halfway through the growing season they put up huge, white nets that let moisture and sunlight come through but kept direct light from hitting the tender plants. Our tasks changed as the tobacco grew, but it always involved being outside in the dirt for long hours. I got along fine with my coworkers—there wasn't any more stealing, at least from me—and I soon observed that the company maintained a standard of excellence. They came by regularly and inspected our work, which tutored me into maturity and kept me performing well. Dad probably had some insight when he told me, "Just stay there a couple more days. You'll get used to it." He probably knew there were lessons for me to learn.

It didn't take many weeks for that tobacco to spring up and become ready for harvest. Right before my eyes I watched the whole sowing-and-reaping cycle take place. That did a lot for me because it put a very vivid image of the principle of sowing and reaping (planting, tending, and harvesting) into my mind. I never forgot it. I had seen cycles of planting before when my granddad grew corn and beans in Georgia, but I hadn't worked the fields with him. Now, the example was right before my eyes.

Without trying, I became a leader of the workers, and our bosses saw that. They observed the work I did and the type of conversation I had, which was different from the others. I didn't see myself the way they saw themselves. I had been brought up in an environment that convinced me I was a king, someone capable of supervising, managing, and leading. When you come into other environments, that royal identity comes out. It is a law, and it does not fail or change. In those tobacco fields, I rose to the top because I saw myself, as I now put it, as royalty.

Just as the prodigal son was tutored by his experience, so those tobacco fields taught me hard work, perseverance, how to get along with people, and many other valuable lessons. But more than anything, I saw how we advance not by toil but by character. Yes, there was hard work involved all summer long, but we all worked hard; I did not advance over others by working harder. I advanced because of how I saw myself, which affected the level of my performance and how others saw me. (See Numbers 13:33.) That is why before I left the tobacco fields, the foreman asked me to come back the next summer to serve as his assistant. I told him I appreciated the offer but I was moving on to other opportunities. I didn't want to spend another summer in those fields!

Toil had not produced favor; character had produced favor. I did not earn it; I received it. I believe God's favor was working in my life before I gave my life to Him. It is very important that we understand that toil does not attain promotion. Toil, which is hard labor with pain and fatigue, is designed to wear us down. God planned for us to live and work like Him, by faith with joy! Promotion comes from the Lord (Ps. 75:6–7), not from painful toil and hard labor. This is a royal principle that will literally change the way you approach your finances, your career, and much more. Let me explain a little more.

No More Toil

Toil, put plainly, is a curse. Jesus has redeemed us from the curse (Gal. 3:13). It was never meant for God's household to live under the curse of toil. But though we have been delivered from toil, toil has been written into our subconscious minds because of the curse. Surprisingly, many of God's children think that if it's not hard, it's not God. Wrong! This is why we must resist the temptation to toil and instead start receiving from our Provider. I call it the "no toil anointing"!

Why does toil still exist? Because while humanity was freed from the curse, the ground was not freed. The curse is still working in the earth; the earth has yet to be redeemed, though one day it will be. You may notice that it doesn't take any effort to make weeds grow in your garden. That's because your garden is still functioning under God's declaration made in Genesis 3:17: "And unto Adam he [God] said, Because thou hast hearkened unto the voice of thy wife, and hast eaten of the tree...cursed is the ground for thy sake."

But while the ground remains cursed, you and I have been freed from the curse. The Bible says, "The just shall live by faith." (See Habakkuk 2:4; Romans 1:17; Galatians 3:11; Hebrews 10:38.) The kingdom of God ushers in a new order of living by faith that shields us from the effects of the curse and elevates us into a revelation of royalty once again. We operate by the higher principles of the kingdom, which dominate the curse. There really are just two choices: operating under the curse or operating by faith. They don't mix. We must choose between them.

A great illustration of this is in the Gospels, where Peter the disciple was operating under a cursed, labor-based mindset. The Bible tells us Peter, a fisherman, had "toiled all the night" and caught nothing. Today most believers are operating in that same system of toil. To most people, toil is the only system that makes any logical sense. You work hard by the sweat of your brow and eke out a living from unforgiving circumstances. But Jesus was about to teach Peter what it looks like to operate by faith instead of toil.

Jesus told this experienced fisherman to "launch out into the deep" in broad daylight, and let down his net "for a catch [of fish]" (Luke 5:4, KJV, AMP). Because Jesus was commanding this, it was literally a word of revelation from God. It could not fail, and it could only be "earned" by obedience. You may know what happened next: Peter and his partners brought in so many fish that their net broke and their boat began to sink. The miraculous catch was so massive it threatened to sink his partners' boats.

Peter was astonished at the number of fish bulging from his net because this was not supposed to happen under a toil-based system. As a result he cried out, "Depart from me; for I am a sinful man, O Lord" (Luke 5:8). You might say this was Peter's aha moment, when two systems—the kingdom and the world, provision and toil—collided right in front of him. Peter didn't work for that catch; he believed for it. Once he obeyed Jesus' command, the word of the kingdom, he tapped into an inexhaustible supply. The abundance was so great, it astonished him and brought Peter to a point of decision.

He had launched out based on nothing more than a word of revelation (called *rhema*) and caught more fish than he had ever caught in one run. Let me repeat: Peter didn't toil or struggle for this big haul. All he had to do was believe the word of Jesus, then act on the word. That was it. Remember, the word of God comes with its own power to fulfill itself.

Peter then repented for a sinful, toiling mindset, which denies the power of the kingdom. From that day forth he began learning to receive by revelation instead of toil.

It was a powerful, life-changing moment for him and surely for the other disciples who were with him.

The effect of this kingdom catch of fish went far beyond those fishermen. When Peter acted on the words of Jesus, his fishing partners didn't just catch enough fish for their families. Their haul was so large that it actually changed the entire economy of that coastal city of Capernaum. Wow! Everything Jesus did was above and beyond the need—and none of it happened by toil. It all happened by revelation.

As the body of Christ, we urgently need to get this revelation deep inside our spirits so that we see more miraculous demonstrations in the church. Once you begin to live by this revelation, God can flow through you, but He can't flow through you if you haven't renewed your mind to kingdom thinking. Toil will get you nowhere with God. But if you meditate on the Word of God concerning provision, doors of abundant supply will open for you in the midst of your assignment, as the door opened for Peter. The provision will come through revelation, not toil, just as God rained down manna from heaven in the wilderness so that all His people had to do was gather it up (Exod. 16). Your faith and obedience will produce provision because of revelation, and like Peter in the boat, your job will be to gather up the overwhelming supply.

You Were Not Designed to Meet Your Own Needs

The heading of this section may surprise you, but it is absolutely true. You were not designed to provide for yourself! You were born to live in Eden, where everything was provided for you. Romans 14:17 describes the kingdom as "righteousness, and peace, and joy in the Holy Ghost." I don't see the words *toil* or *sweat* in there. Eden is a type of heaven on the earth, a place not only of luxury and opulence but of unbroken peace and unending joy. What the world calls "work" is the enemy's design to enslave or even kill us. This is because we tend to equate work with toil and our assignment with our provision. Those things are not connected in God's royal household.

God told Adam, "I have given you every herb-bearing seed—everything you'll ever need—and to you it shall be for meat [or provision]." (See Genesis 1:29.) In other words, God said, "You don't need to struggle for anything. Here it is. I have already provided."

Only after Adam sinned did he and Eve try to provide for themselves. We know this because they sewed fig-leaf suits to cover themselves. (See Genesis 3:7.) But even after their fall, the Bible says, "The LORD God made tunics of [animal] skins for Adam and his wife and clothed them" (Gen. 3:21, AMP). God stepped in to provide for them as a demonstration that mankind was not intended to provide for itself.

The world's system of toil says you must work for everything you have. The system of the kingdom says you must believe for everything you have. As strange as it may sound to some, your job has nothing to do with your prosperity. God supplies your needs independent of your job. He assigns us work to release our potential. We should never depend on a job to meet our needs. God wants to be our only source and supply. Adam didn't earn his living before the fall, and we shouldn't either now that Jesus has redeemed us from the curse.

Let me say it another way. Unfortunately, most Christian folks still try to make things work by sweating it out. They confuse assignments (colaboring with God by faith, empowered by grace) with toil. They define work (which God designed to release our potential) as laboring hard and painfully to achieve what God freely gives us. The devil knows that God wants to take care of you, but God can take care of you only when you believe Him and exercise your faith, as Peter did. The enemy's goal is to hold you in his system and cause you to become fearful of leaving it. He will try every trick he can to keep you out of faith and in hard labor.

The revelation of royalty shows us a whole new way of living—a lifestyle without limits. This kingdom lifestyle says there are no financial impossibilities because God can solve any financial problem overnight. This is depicted all throughout the Bible. When God provided Abraham a ram to sacrifice instead of Isaac, his son, the Scripture says, "And Abraham called the name of that place Jehovahjireh [that is, The LORD will provide]" (Gen. 22:14, KJ21). Abraham didn't provide his own ram—God did. Abraham experienced the *berakah*, or blessing of the Lord, and because of it, he no longer had to make things happen through toil. Divine favor, success, riches, and supernatural empowerment worked on his behalf because Abraham became fully persuaded that what God had promised, He was also able to perform (Rom. 4:21).

Similarly, the Israelites did as Moses instructed and asked the Egyptians for articles of silver and gold and for clothing. The Lord had made the Egyptians favorably disposed toward the people, and they gave them what they asked for, so they plundered the Egyptians (Exod. 12:35–36). Not even sickness could touch their bodies because "He brought them forth also with silver and gold: and there was not one feeble person among their tribes" (Ps. 105:37).

For forty years the Lord was with Moses and the children of Israel and they "lacked nothing" (Deut. 2:7). Even their clothes and shoes never wore out, as it says, "And I have led you forty years in the wilderness: your clothes are not waxen old upon you, and thy shoe is not waxen old upon thy foot" (Deut. 29:5).

God provided everything they needed for the journey. He also protected them, fought their battles, and made their enemies to fear them. How much more will God provide and protect you and me?

How about the widow with two sons in 2 Kings 4, who cried out to the prophet Elisha? Her sons were about to be forcibly taken from her and put into bondage by the creditors. Through wisdom, the man of God directed her to a seed already in her house (a jar of oil), which supernaturally supplied her with a harvest sufficient for her to pay her debt and live off the rest—without toil.

God has already provided everything you and I will ever need according to life and godliness until Jesus comes (2 Pet. 1:3). God has done all He is going to do about our salvation, our finances, our healing, our businesses, our families, and so on. Our part is to believe and receive His provision.

THE STORY OF MISS LOVE

When Veronica and I moved to Tulsa, Oklahoma, where I attended seminary, it was close to Christmastime. Although we were not yet familiar with the city, we decided to sow groceries to a family in need. After we went shopping, we loaded the car with bags of food and drove off, under the guidance of the Holy Ghost, toward a government housing project to find someone to bless.

After a few stops we were finally directed to Miss Love, who lived in a small apartment on the second floor. Her daughter was on drugs, and she was taking care of her small grandkids. She had just run out of food, and as I recall, the only thing left in her refrigerator was a jar of water.

When I knocked on her door and told her that I was a minister and had some groceries for her, she flung open the door, shouting to her grandkids, "See, babies, I told you God was going to bring us something to eat." And He did!

Miss Love had no money to give, but she sowed the seed of faith and reaped a harvest during her time of need. God provided for her without her toiling. In faith she postured herself to receive supernaturally.

In His kingdom economy God teaches us to take no anxious thought for our life, what we're going to eat or drink. All of these things do the Gentiles seek (Matt. 6:31–32). "But seek ye first the kingdom of God, and his righteousness; and all these things shall be added unto you" (v. 33).

You and I are here not only to enforce a royal government but to establish this royal economy. God's plan

from the beginning has been for us to become a generation of leaders governing by revelation of the kingdom
of God. There is no financial shortage or lack in the
kingdom of God. The law of seedtime and harvest, of
receiving instead of toiling, works for anyone with faith.
This royal kingdom is independent of, and superior to,
this world's system.

If the devil can keep you believing in toil, you will
remain in bondage to his system. The moment you
switch systems to God's economy, Satan can no longer
keep you down. You are not under his feet—the devil is
under your feet (Rom. 16:20)!

LIVING IN SURVIVAL MODE

Unlike Miss Love, many Christians act like survivors
even after they have been rescued. That is, they live
each day simply trying to survive instead of thriving
by entering into the promises of God that Jesus died to
give us. Adam became a survivor on the earth after he
sinned. He was now out of fellowship with God, his provider. Having lost his provision, Adam was forced to
scratch, struggle, and sweat for everything he got. Even
worse than that, he was put out of the garden and lost his
assignment.

I know what it feels like to be in survival mode,
because I had to attend survival school while serving in
the military. During this training, I was taken into the
woods with others, and some were dressed as the enemy.
This exercise occurred at night, and those in enemy
clothing would chase the rest of us and shoot at us with
guns loaded with blanks. We were also taught what to

eat and what not to eat because some plants in the woods are poisonous and can kill you if eaten. It was a hectic way to live, having to provide for your own needs all the time and being chased by pretend foes.

Sadly, most people today live in some level of survival mode because they are hooked on toil and just trying to stay alive. To be provision-minded means to leave our royal assignments by the wayside. We prioritize paychecks over power, retirement benefits over the blessing of God. When money preoccupies your mind, the gifts that God placed inside of you go undeveloped. You don't value that part of your life. You are thinking only about money. Instead of focusing on your gifts, you focus on working a job to meet your needs.

This creates tragic results. When a God assignment presents itself, survivors say, "Oh, I'd love to do that, but I have to get a job so I can make some money." Or they may say, "That job with that company doesn't pay enough, so I will stay where I am," even though God has assigned them to a new place. If we are not postured to listen and receive without the stress of surviving, we may not perceive that the lower-paying job is the location of our next assignment, the place where God strategically wants to place us. God may be using that assignment to develop your gift or to reach someone through you. Maybe the CEO or another employee is ready to hear the gospel. Toiling for provision keeps us in bondage to Satan's system and blinds us to what God wants to do through our lives.

People often come to church because they are looking for a solution to a "provision" issue. When they get there, they find that the people in the church are struggling just as much as they are, so they leave without the issue being resolved. Many churches are large groups of people surviving and toiling rather than walking in the blessing of royal provision.

Again, we were not created to connect our jobs or our long work hours to how God wishes to provide for us. That is a distortion, and that distorted image has been placed in us by the enemy. Jesus came to destroy that image and get us connected to heaven's economy.

A MIGRATORY MINDSET

Provision-mindedness makes you migratory as well. You always feel the need to go somewhere else to meet your needs or to get more. Professionals act this way just as much as anyone else. "That job pays more. I have to move to that city." It's a poverty mindset dressed up as promotion. If you don't have enough financially, the world tells you to get two jobs or three jobs. That's the beckoning call of your slave master, who wants to control and steal your life by making toiling for provision seem like the only honorable option. But God says your gift will make room for you and bring you before great men. You don't have to toil to achieve His will!

I went through a toiling, migratory phase early in my career at IBM. When I got to that company, sales were down industry-wide, and I didn't know how to sell computers. I was still learning, so "just to be safe" I got a second job working after-hours at a furniture store in another part of town. I would finish at IBM at 5 o'clock, then rush south of town to work in the furniture store.

My mind was in total survivor mode. I always wanted to have a backup plan, but I was running my mind and body ragged. That's what toil does—it wears you down and causes mental fatigue, making you less productive and creative. By Sundays, I was exhausted.

Then one day at IBM a secretary said out of the blue, "I believe if you want to, you can work this job and it can be everything you want it to be." She was referring to my two-job schedule and the harm it was doing me. That was a key insight, and when she made that comment, it clicked. I was wasting energy by channeling it in two directions rather than focusing it powerfully in one direction. I was hedging my bets and weakening my results.

I took that advice, quit the furniture store, and rapidly became a leading salesman at IBM. Even then I had to stay steady and not get into toil in the form of overwork, because if the subconscious mind is not transformed, it will find a way to toil even though we have been redeemed from it. This is a significant point. Your subconscious mind will keep you in line with what you really believe. If you actually believe in the value of toil, your mind will pull you back in that direction. If you think you have to work harder to buy a better house or send your kids to a better school, you are still functioning in a toiling mindset. It needs to be broken continually until receiving becomes your normal method of provision.

It may help you to remind yourself of how salvation works. We are saved by grace through faith, and that not of ourselves; it is the gift of God, not of works

(Eph. 2:8–9). You don't work for salvation. Salvation is already given to you. It is a gift. If salvation is a free gift, why would the rest of the kingdom lifestyle operate any other way?

In Genesis 12, God told Abram (before his name was changed to Abraham), "I am going to bless you. I'm going to make your name great, and you're going to be a blessing. As a matter of fact, I'm going to bless those that bless you and curse him that curses you. Through you shall all the families of the earth be blessed." (See verses 2–3.) He did not say, "Toil long enough and hard enough, and I will bless you; the more you toil, the more you will be blessed." No way!

Remember when Jesus said, "Blessed be ye poor: for yours is the kingdom of God" (Luke 6:20)? He was saying that by receiving this new kingdom, you are blessed because you can now live and operate by the new economy of the kingdom of God, which gives you access to unlimited heavenly provision. Religious tradition teaches that Jesus was saying the poor are blessed because they are God's favorites, and they will get theirs in the sweet by-and-by when they die and go to heaven. No! Jesus was teaching that poverty is under the curse, and now that the kingdom has come, you'll never have to be broke another day in your life. This is why Jesus told the disciples to tell John the Baptist, "And the poor have the gospel preached to them" (Matt. 11:5). The good news is that you don't need to be poor anymore!

EMPOWERED TO PROSPER

Survivors act like God dropped us on this earth without any help or heavenly assistance, which is totally contrary to the gospel. When Jesus was about to leave this earth and return to the Father, He told His disciples (and us), "I will pray the Father, and he shall give you another Comforter, that he may abide with you for ever....I will not leave you comfortless" (John 14:16, 18). Jesus was talking about the Holy Spirit, whom God sent on the day of Pentecost. "And suddenly there came a sound from heaven as of a rushing mighty wind.... And there appeared unto them cloven tongues like as of fire....And they were all filled with the Holy Ghost" (Acts 2:2–4).

The Holy Spirit brings God's power to bear in our lives—"But ye shall receive power, after that the Holy Ghost is come upon you" (Acts 1:8)—to manifest what God wants done in the earth. What kind of Comforter would the Holy Ghost be if He did not provide for us? The revelation of royalty is great comfort to the people of God. Our King provides for us. You don't have to toil or wrestle anymore for a living. We serve a good God. As Christians, we are more than just followers of Christ. We are members of the royal household, sons and daughters of God, those "to whom God would make known what is the riches of the glory of this mystery among the Gentiles; which is Christ in you, the hope of glory" (Col. 1:27).

WITHOUT WEALTH, YOUR ROYALTY IS IN QUESTION

This chapter would not be complete without talking about the wealth that God has for the body of Christ. The Babylonian (world) system has tried to impoverish the church and strip it of its identity. But God plans for the church to be the most powerful and wealthiest institution on the planet. He knows that when people witness heaven's wealth manifested through God's people, "all the nations in the world shall see that you belong to the Lord, and they will stand in awe" (Deut. 28:10, TLB).

One man of God said that without wealth, your royalty as a child of God is in question. This statement might offend some, but God's children were born into a royal family, and the Father's wealth extends to the Father's children. Too many Christians have been discouraged from using their faith to prosper, but the Scriptures are clear that God is not only OK with us prospering, but He will also help us in the process. I have never seen a poor king. Have you? Part of a king's glory is the wealth of his kingdom. It is also part of God's glory.

Here is how the queen of Sheba responded when she saw King Solomon's royal court:

> When the queen of Sheba saw all the wisdom of Solomon and the palace he had built, the food on his table, the seating of his officials, the attending servants in their robes, his cupbearers, and the burnt offerings he made at the temple of the LORD, she

was overwhelmed. She said to the king, "The report I heard in my own country about your achievements and your wisdom is true. But I did not believe these things until I came and saw with my own eyes. Indeed, not even half was told me; in wisdom and wealth you have far exceeded the report I heard."

—1 KINGS 10:4–7, NIV

Wealth is part of your royal identity, and you must be bold and courageous in believing God for it.

CHAPTER 9

FROM INFORMATION
TO REVELATION

✦————————————————✦

W E RECEIVE FROM God not by information but by revelation. There is a world of difference.

One great historical example is the famous African American agricultural scientist George Washington Carver. Carver called his laboratory "God's Little Workshop." There, he discovered more than three hundred uses for the peanut, including face powder, instant coffee, and paints. Carver's method was this: he would close the door and listen to God. He would bring no books into his laboratory. God gave him creative ideas that unlocked the secrets of this humble plant. Carver said, "The Great Creator taught me to take the peanut apart and put it together again."[1] Carver's ability to hear God and follow His instruction regarding agriculture helped to change the economy of the southern United States in the early 1900s.

There is no trial and error in the kingdom. Revelation is always right on!

REVELATION BY DESIGN

Dr. Carver was functioning by humanity's original design. This is your design as well—it is available to you right now. Like Adam before he sinned, you have a direct line of communication with God through your spirit. God's desire is to constantly give you revelation or grace knowledge as you walk through life. This is knowledge that comes by faith through the Holy Spirit. It is not learned; it is discerned.

That's how Adam was able to name all of the animals. He was connected to God, walking in faith and fellowship with Him. He perceived what God thought and what God liked. When it came time for Adam to name the animals, he downloaded the names from God—or rather, he knew them without effort, because Adam and God were not two; they were one. Jesus said, "I and my Father are one" (John 10:30). Paul wrote that you and I are one spirit with Him now, having been redeemed from the curse (1 Cor. 6:17; Gal. 3:13). The original plan is back in operation.

Once Adam sinned, that instant, perfect connection was broken. Adam went from revelation to information—functioning by what he could receive through his five senses. However, that was not his—or our—original culture. Eden is our original culture. God did not want His family to be a bunch of intellectuals operating by natural information. He wanted a people dependent on the "higher education" of the kingdom of God to supply all their needs. Notice that there weren't any schools in the Garden of Eden, no educational systems, no books.

To struggle and toil for answers is the culture of fallen humanity.

Adam was taught through the anointing and functioned by revelation. He did not earn or attain the revelation of that higher kingdom—and neither do we. It is simply given and received. We don't have to scratch and claw for it; it is freely provided.

PEOPLE WHO FUNCTIONED BY REVELATION

History and the Bible provide many other examples of men and women who functioned by revelation rather than information. I remember renowned surgeon Dr. Ben Carson telling how during one particularly challenging surgery, the patient's brain stem was bleeding profusely and Carson didn't know what to do. He prayed, "Lord, it's up to You. You've got to do something here....[This patient] will die unless You show me what to do." Within seconds, he said, "a kind of intuitive knowledge" filled his mind, and he knew exactly what to do.[2] Carson was walking in the revelation of God.

Revelation turned another man, Gideon, into the leader of a successful army. Before that revelation arrived, Gideon was the least in his household and belonged to the most insignificant family in his tribe. He had never been trained to lead an army. (See Judges 6.) Revelation promotes and advances people who lack what the world deems necessary information. Revelation puts on display God's superior method of leadership: "But God chose the foolish things of the world to shame the wise" (1 Cor. 1:27, NIV).

In this same way, the Holy Spirit directed the

missionary work of the apostle Paul by revelation. "Paul and his companions traveled throughout the region of Phrygia and Galatia, having been kept by the Holy Spirit from preaching the word in the province of Asia. When they came to the border of Mysia, they tried to enter Bithynia, but the Spirit of Jesus would not allow them to" (Acts 16:6–7, NIV). That is a picture of God superseding logical information and guiding by revelation.

Of course, our perfect example is Jesus, who said, "I tell you the truth: the Son can do nothing on his own; he does only what he sees his Father doing. What the Father does, the Son also does" (John 5:19, GNT). This is revelation talk, not information talk. Jesus walked in perfect obedience to revelation, and it equipped Him to launch a ministry like the world had never seen.

In Genesis, Joseph's God-given wisdom and ability to interpret dreams took him from a prison cell to the king's palace and made him famous and distinguished. No amount of information could have done that; it was all revelation. Years later in a different world empire, Daniel similarly rose to almost unparalleled power simply by sharing the revelations given to him by God.

God desires to do the same thing for you. Just as Joseph and Daniel were planted in godless empires, members of the body of Christ are planted in this dark world to bring hope and provide solutions in challenging times. "Ye are the light of the world" (Matt. 5:14). God's plan for us, His royal children, is that we would create a platform of such credibility that the world would inquire about our family and our Father. Neither Pharaoh nor Nebuchadnezzar inquired about the one true God until

Joseph and Daniel, respectively, solved their personal and national problems—through divine revelation.

As the Garden of Eden supplied everything for Adam, the government of God is going to supply everything, including revelation, that you need to prosper in your assignment.

UNREASONABLE ACTIONS

Some experts estimate that knowledge and technology are doubling every twelve to thirteen months.[3] That is a breathtaking reality, but in practical terms, how would anyone keep up with all that information? You can't read enough books, and you don't have enough hours. Information is plentiful, but revelation is price- less. Revelation goes far beyond information. Revelation is based on principles, not data. It works at a whole different and higher level. It comes from above. A life governed by revelation can respond effectively to any cir- cumstance and challenge, while a life governed by infor- mation is drastically limited. Ultimately we don't need more data; we need to hear from God about what to do. Even Albert Einstein said, "The significant problems we face cannot be solved at the same level of thinking we were at when we created them."[4]

Everything God does is unreasonable according to our earthly standards. It transcends logic and therefore looks foolish. God has His own standard of what's reasonable, and it is based on eternal, supernatural standards, not what the worldly mind of man can comprehend. Satan's wisdom is based in information, earth-bound, and seem- ingly logical. God's wisdom is supernatural, eternal, and unstoppable. It doesn't always look right at first, but it always does right. Jesus said, "Wisdom is justified by her children" (Matt. 11:19, KJ21).

You will always serve the one that provides for you. If information, toil, and struggle are your providers, then you are their slave. But if God's revelation provides for you, then you are His son or daughter. People on earth must choose to be supplied by one kingdom or the other. The wise and godly will learn to get their provisions from outside of this world's system via revelation. Jesus said this about money:

> The light of the body is the eye: if therefore thine eye be single, thy whole body shall be full of light. But if thine eye be evil, thy whole body shall be full of darkness. If therefore the light that is in thee be darkness, how great is that darkness! No man can serve two masters: for either he will hate the one, and love the other; or else he will hold to the one, and despise the other. Ye cannot serve God and mammon.
>
> —MATTHEW 6:22–24

YOU ARE EMPOWERED TO SUCCEED

As a believer, you have already been supplied by God with everything you will ever need to be effective and productive. Your part is to consistently operate not through stress or toil but through revelation—connecting with God, looking to Him, talking with Him, and seeking His perspective. Divine guidance and revelation will guarantee excellence and right decisions in all your earthly challenges and pursuits. Once you operate this way, your life will become distinctly different from what it was before and different from the lives of those around you who are functioning merely by information.

Revelation dramatically lifts you up and promotes you to the top, no matter what your color or country, industry or field of endeavor. It makes no difference what socio-economic group you were born into or if you even know your biological parents. When revelation comes on your life, your status will start to change instantly. Get ready! It's your season to move to the top: "the LORD shall make thee the head, and not the tail; and thou shalt be above only, and thou shalt not be beneath" (Deut. 28:13).

The higher we climb in rank or responsibility, the more crucial it becomes that we, the children of God, hear and follow the direction of God. Many times there is a price to pay for making right decisions or doing what is right in God's eyes. But His vindication is sure, and His rewards are great. He promises that those who follow His commands "shall not be ashamed" (Rom. 10:11). *The Message* says, "No one who trusts God like this—heart and soul—will ever regret it."

The enemy traffics in dark knowledge, which is worldly wisdom and natural information. In this way he tries to keep people locked below the line, functioning in the natural realm without heavenly help. All knowledge apart from God is dark knowledge, even if it comes with a PhD.

One example from Scripture is the rich young ruler who asked Jesus how to receive eternal life (Matt. 19:16–22). He had heard Jesus preach about it, but this eternal life Jesus spoke of went against all earthly logic. Jesus received a revelation that this man needed to give away his worldly possessions so he could begin operating by revelation. This man was certainly well educated and probably the equivalent of a CEO with an MBA. But he was functioning below the line in the realm of limited vision, provision, and toil. He actually had a survivor mentality, though he was very wealthy. He could not understand a method of provision that came from above.

Here's something to remember: revelation or grace knowledge allows you to see the full spectrum of reality, not just what is visible but also what is invisible.

KINGS' KIDS DON'T BEG

Even within the body of Christ a culture of toiling can develop. I have even heard people say you have to struggle for revelation. It is hard to receive revelation from God with the wrong image.

To explain, let me share a personal experience I had many years ago when I was first starting in the ministry. We were living in Minnesota, and one Saturday night at about midnight I was trying to get a message to preach Sunday morning. I cried out, "God, I need a message. The people have to have a message." I seemed to be praying, but in reality I was bawling, squalling, and begging. "God, I don't have a message for tomorrow. Please, God!" I went on and on like this.

After a while a voice said to my heart, "What are you doing?" That caught me up short! Wasn't it obvious what I was doing?

"Trying to get a message," I responded, very reasonably.

"Is that the way you come before Me?" He asked.

"No," I said, half-guessing.

"How do you come before Me?" He asked.

"The Scripture says to come boldly before the throne of grace," I said.

His message to me was clear: straighten up and quit begging! As soon as I approached Him the biblical way, the sermon started to flow from God into my spirit. I almost couldn't write it down fast enough. Begging and cajoling had accomplished nothing, while faith and boldness accomplished everything.

I learned several lessons that night. First, as I said, it's hard to receive from God when you have the wrong image. Second, God has a royal protocol for how we, as His royal children, are to approach Him. And third, often we don't have because we ask amiss or out of line with the kingdom.

Our Father doesn't like His kids to come to Him begging and crying. His mercy can cover that, but He knows when you're ready to grow up. We are not beggars—we are children! God does not respond to begging; He responds to faith. This principle has flooded my ministry with revelation and kept me from approaching God the wrong way on many occasions. Just as I believed for a sermon that night, I have to believe for everything God provides. I have to believe for my healing. I have to believe for the money to operate our facilities and staff. I have to believe for my clothes, my increase, my promotion—everything.

Believe me, that begging mentality is a spirit that is always standing by to draw you back in. After all, begging makes sense to the natural mind. But if you let that

137

spirit get on you, you will always be begging. That's just not the way God wants it. He wants you to get your needs met from the inside, by faith and revelation. This pleases Him.

Not only does begging not work; it also sets a sad example for the kingdom. It makes people think that our kingdom is broke, our Father is weak, and our calling is unsure. The kingdom is not broke, our Father is not weak, and our calling is not unsure! When we portray the kingdom, our Father, and our calling as ineffective, which we do whenever we beg, we misrepresent our royalty and malign the character of our Sovereign. Rather, we should stand up in righteousness, speaking the revelations of God over our situations. That's what David did when he faced Goliath. He came up to the front line and found all the Israelite soldiers hiding from that giant and speaking from a perspective of fear. The victory belonged to the one who had received revelation from heaven about the fate of that foe. David operated by revelation, not begging and pleading.

Revelation gives us boldness. We have to see ourselves the way God sees us. God does not see us as broke beggars. He sees us as royalty, children of the Most High who own the whole earth (Ps. 82:6). The Word says the righteous are as bold as a lion. God will supply your needs just like He will supply mine, every time.

Begging also leads us into a welfare mentality. Begging people always want a handout, something for nothing, someone else to take care of their needs. I travel to different countries preaching on this revelation of royalty, and for some reason many of the people in those places are entrenched in a welfare mentality, always looking for a handout. They seem to think that the God of America is different from the God of Uganda or the God of Australia or the God of some other country. They send me letters asking for money. They approach me in person to ask for help with some need. Even if I helped them, it would not be God's best for them. They need to learn to function by revelation of the kingdom of God, not handouts. They shouldn't be looking for welfare but should be expecting to fare well because the kingdom has come (Matt. 5:3).

Only orphans act like they don't have a Daddy to guide and provide for them. It's time for the body of Christ to stop acting as if we have no heavenly Father who reveals things to His children. There's no lack of money or revelation or brilliant ideas in the kingdom of God. Start thinking like God thinks, because "as [a man] thinketh in his heart, so is he" (Prov. 23:7).

BREAKING BARRIERS

Switching from information to revelation means breaking a barrier in our thinking, and this usually involves a whole lot of discomfort. When you approach that barrier, everything around you may look like it's starting to shake. Breaking through the barrier requires changes in your relationships, your manner of operation, and your habits. It means becoming open to unexpected solutions and provision. I like how someone put it: "When you start walking in revelation, get ready to receive foolish thoughts," thoughts that are foolish to the intellect and natural mind.

I often use the example of when man first broke the sound barrier to illustrate what it takes to break through these kinds of barriers in our thinking. Chuck Yeager was the test pilot who broke the sound barrier on October 14, 1947. Chuck faced plenty of challenges on his way to doing what some said was impossible. He had to face his own fear. Some people thought he was going to disintegrate. Others were probably jealous of him and did not want him to attempt it.

When Chuck flew his jet faster and faster, approaching the sound barrier, everything on the jet began to shake. But in the next moment, he broke through the sound barrier and everything smoothed out.[5] This is a great illustration of what it takes to break off the bondage of toil and informational thinking. You can tell you are breaking through that barrier because everything around you looks like it's shaking. But if you stay on course, God will take you through, and on the other side is smooth sailing—a life lived by a flow of revelation from above.

I experienced this when I first started to tithe. Giving 10 percent of my income to the church made me so uncomfortable that I felt shaken! I would say to myself, "Man, I sure hope this works." I had never done anything like that before. It was a real barrier, but I diligently obeyed, and God taught me how to give. I was living by His superior revelation, and the sense of shaking stopped.

Wouldn't you know it, then God stretched me again in my giving. He would lead me (by revelation) to give a certain amount above my tithe to a church I was visiting or to give a certain amount to a ministry. Each of those barriers caused some shaking, but I am happy to say that now it is much easier for me to give. His revelation and faithfulness led me through those barriers. A few years ago my wife and I gave more away than what I made through my paycheck. That was the first time we had ever done that. Another barrier—broken!

Every barrier you break is designed for your increase. It is designed for your promotion. It is designed to get you listening to revelation more than to information. Sure, the enemy will resist and buffet you as best he can during that shaking time, but when you break through to smooth sailing, God will elevate you. He'll take you up higher than you were before.

Joseph in Genesis received prophetic dreams and a coat of many colors from his father, Jacob. The colorful coat prophetically represented the many populations of the world. Joseph was thriving under many promises, but Joseph's brothers, because of jealousy, treated him shamefully, selling him into slavery. What he experienced during the next number of years no doubt tested his revelation of royalty. But God was with Joseph everywhere he went—from the slave pit to Potiphar's house to a prison cell and eventually to the palace, which was his destiny.

The enemy works 24/7, through negative circumstances and unfair situations, to steal your royal identity. He wants to keep you from receiving your rich inheritance that comes only through your royal identity, which is the image of God in you. But when hard times come, do what Joseph did and remain faithful and keep following after God.

Eventually Joseph saw that God was preparing him

to serve as second-in-command to Pharaoh and was building a revelation of royalty into him through circumstances and tasks. Challenges seem to shake and quake us, but when we break through them, clinging confidently and holding steadfast to God's revelation, the experiences actually reinforce our royal pedigree.

This happened to me in Hazardville, where I was forced to break through barriers of potential resentment, fatigue, and anger to rise into my God-given image. God assigned me to work in those tobacco fields so He could take me where He needed me to be next. It was more than a summer job; it was a prearranged assignment. Ephesians 2:10 says our paths are arranged beforehand. God knew the stops I needed to make so I would behave like the royalty He made me to be.

Remember, your inheritance comes only in proportion to your new identity, and your identity comes by revelation. As you receive more knowledge of what it looks like to be a child of God, a member of the royal family, you will be amazed by the number and quality of godly ideas you receive. It's not that God doesn't want to give you every idea He has for you right away, but your image cannot and will not receive them properly unless you move higher and are ready to receive greater revelation. As you go from faith to faith and glory to glory (Rom. 1:17; 2 Cor. 3:18), you are able to receive more of your inheritance.

"And Jabez called on the God of Israel, saying, Oh that thou wouldest bless me indeed, and enlarge my coast, and that thine hand might be with me" (1 Chron. 4:10). I believe Jabez was asking God to increase his capacity to receive God's thoughts—revelation knowledge.

When I returned from Hazardville, I was different. I had broken through a barrier. I could be trusted with more, even though I was still a young man. I could bear responsibility and it wouldn't break me. That environment developed character in me. People who hadn't seen me in a while said, "You really changed this summer."

Expect God to give you, as He gave Daniel, a "ten times better" anointing of wisdom (Dan. 1:20), which will reveal better ways of doing things to help solve humanity's problems. Like Dr. Carver, expect an abundance of creative ideas, new inventions, and world-changing innovations to move you into a place of dominance in your field, profession, or industry. The end result is to advance and establish God's kingdom everywhere you are sent—through ongoing revelation from above.

EXPLOSIVE RESULTS

Revelation comes through meditating on God's Word, which appeals to both your understanding and your imagination. Like seeds, the Word comes with the ability to bring itself to pass. As you meditate on the Word, it produces faith to accomplish what you desire. While information is confined to an earthly level of increase, revelation produces explosive (supernatural) increase. As one man said, revelation brings a revolution.

Consider Jesus' first public miracle, the turning of water into wine (John 2:1–11). He bypassed everything in the natural process to make wine. In the natural, to produce fine wine requires years of planting, growing, harvesting, and aging. The informational route would have literally taken a lifetime. But within seconds Jesus implemented the revelation from the Father by faith and overrode time and nature. He turned mere water into the best and most expensive wine at the wedding. That is an explosive result.

In Genesis 26, Abraham's son Isaac harvested a hundred times more crops than he planted in the same year, during a time of famine, because the Lord said, "I will bless thee, and I will be with thee." (See verses 3 and 12.) This was a miracle, an unnatural, explosive increase that happened in an extremely accelerated fashion.

Revelation will do the same in your life when you make the choice to live by revelation, not information. Don't be a provision-minded survivor chasing money in a migratory way. Decide to step up in confidence like David did, breaking through every barrier on your way to greater levels of accomplishment. Be prepared to receive by revelation multimillion-dollar ideas, benefits and promotions, prosperous visions and dreams, inventions and strategies, progress and divine health, freedom from debt, longevity and fruitfulness, accelerated growth and development, strategic positioning, a new way of living, a new way of thinking, and a new way of working.

You were born for this.

CHAPTER 10

THE WEALTHY BELIEVER

❖———————————————❖

Even when we are walking faithfully with the Lord, we may not always hear Him the first time He speaks. That certainly happened to me when He began telling us to move the location of our church.

It started when one of our members came up to me one day and said, "I saw a little place in Forest Park, and it looked just right for us."

Forest Park was a nearby area that was certainly nicer than where we were—but I was not interested in moving. I dismissed her suggestion as politely as I could. She came up to me again two weeks later.

"Pastor, the Lord keeps speaking to me about that other location, and I really believe you need to see it," she said. This probably took some courage on her part because I clearly wasn't interested, but to quiet her down, I told her I would drive over there and have a look. That's all I committed to do.

I didn't hurry, but I did drive by the property. It was an office building with multiple floors. I was just curious enough to wonder who was the real estate agent in charge of renting it. I contacted that person and met him at the property. The building hall was much more space than we presently needed and a huge jump from where we were. In the natural it didn't make much sense, but I couldn't quite close the door on it yet.

"How much does this place rent for?" I asked the agent.

"Three thousand a month," he said. He may as well have said $3 million. We were paying $562 at the time for the tiny room we met in. "No way," I thought. "I'm sure that's the end of this whole thing."

We completed our tour and went outside, and I was preparing to shake his hand and walk away when I heard God say, "Take it," just as plain as day. The Lord continued His instruction: "Ask if you can use it for Sunday and Wednesday services." We weren't even off the property yet when I turned around and told the agent we would take it! I could hardly believe the sound of my own words.

"My goodness, what have I done?" I wondered while driving home. "This is way beyond us."

Nevertheless, I announced to the congregation that the church would be moving, and right away I began hearing from members who did not want to move with us! They said they felt called to stay, and I respected that, even if I thought some of them should come with us. When everything shook out, only around fifteen members were making the move with us. We were growing and shrinking at the same time!

"Oh, my Lord," I prayed, "what are we going to do?" I was thinking revenue, bills, rent, expenses. "How are we going to pay everything involved with this new place with just fifteen people?"

I couldn't see a way in the natural, and after hearing me out, God was faithful to speak to me. He said, "Whom do you trust—Me or them?"

I said, "You, Lord."

He then told me a couple of things: Number one, people were not to be our source. Number two, He could meet our needs by many or by few. (See 1 Samuel 14:6.) This was encouraging to me. At that point I had two options— believe God or believe what I saw in the natural realm. There was no way I was going back to living below the line, so Veronica and I started declaring our destiny and legislating our future: "Thank You, Lord, that we have three services full on Sunday mornings." Did we have three services on Sunday morning? No, we barely had half a service! But we decided not to believe our natural eyes but our eyes of faith. We spoke royal words into the problematic situation, knowing that faith words are seeds of promise that would soon grow.

Ecclesiastes 8:4 says, "Where the word of a king is, there is power." We decreed these things often: "Thank You that people are lined up down the sidewalk, waiting to get into the next service." At first nothing visible happened. We still had fifteen people in the congregation, meeting in a much larger facility, but we continued to declare the future week after week, calling things that were not as though they were.

I also resolved not to pressure the people for more money. I would not take up endless offerings or put a table in front and say, "I'm counting here, and we need someone to give more." I never wanted to get into manipulation, gimmicks, or begging because none of that is royalty. Rather, I knew the Word of God and the Spirit of God would motivate people to give.

That is exactly what happened. Almost as soon as we announced that we were moving, money began coming in from people who weren't even in our church! God opened sources of supply that I didn't even know were there. It was simply amazing to us and very encouraging. Our team was excited, and a great group was forming a foundation for future ministry together.

I am happy to say that due to God's provision, we were never late on the rent. In fact the real estate agent who rented it to us came to one of our services and gave his life to the Lord. He became so confident that we would always pay on time that he later said, "I can set my clock by the rent money coming in from this ministry." That's a royal compliment!

INCREASE

We entered a new season in which God added steadily to our church family. Soon we weren't just declaring three services and a line waiting to get in—we were seeing it in the natural. Each time a service filled up, we added another one, eight hundred people per service. We put chairs in the lobby and out in the hall. It seemed like chairs were everywhere. People were packed in to hear the Word of God.

All of this was done by faith, not human effort. It was about God's kingdom being built as He ordained it. Veronica and I simply stood on the promises God had given us. He told us through His Word that He would not let us be ashamed. He promised us that whatever we did would prosper. He promised us that He would be with us always. We stood on so many promises! When you confess the Word, it first changes your image, and then it changes your circumstances. This is God's way. It is His order of operation. Once your image is changed, your reality changes as well.

God's work among us was becoming conspicuous. One of the city officials came by to see me one weekday and said, "Reverend, what are you doing here? People are lined up all the way down the street. What is going on in there?" Maybe he wanted some explanation or apology. All I said was, "The Word is going forth." That was the truth. God was speaking. Half the stuff I preached on Sundays were things I didn't even plan on preaching. I would prepare a message as best I could, and then the people listening that morning would pull something else out of me by the Spirit. The Holy Ghost always knows what your audience needs to hear. He knows who's coming to each service and how He wants to change their lives. It was an awesome thing to watch Him at work.

Still, the city council was increasingly concerned, and they contacted me again. Imagine being upset that people wanted to learn about God and be better parents, employees, business owners, and citizens!

"You're taking up all the parking spaces nearby," they told me. "What exactly is going on in there?"

I decided to play with them a little bit.

"I'm fixing a good meal," I replied. "People need

something good to eat, and the Word of God is the food people need."

They didn't bother me after that.

THE INFLUENCE OF AFFLUENCE

When God is truly at work, you won't be able to hide it. Royalty doesn't rule in secret but openly. Jesus called His kingdom a city on a hill (Matt. 5:14), a beautiful, powerful capital that everybody sees and respects. When your royalty is operating, God will raise you up in front of your community—you can count on it. Why? God promised this to Abraham and his seed, which includes you and me.

> And I will make you a great nation, and I will bless you [abundantly], and make your name great (exalted, distinguished); and you shall be a blessing [a source of great good to others]; and I will bless (do good for, benefit) those who bless you, and I will curse [that is, subject to My wrath and judgment] the one who curses (despises, dishonors, has contempt for) you. And in you all the families (nations) of the earth will be blessed.
>
> —GENESIS 12:2–3, AMP

The image of royalty will also affect your finances. Our church had learned valuable lessons at the bottom of the financial ladder, and now we were learning to go higher into the influence of affluence. God is a big thinker, and He wants us to think big like He does. God provided abundantly for everything we did. He pays your expenses so He can display His affluence. He is a wealthy

God, and so are His offspring. Any affluence God gives you is to lead you to influence others to know Him. His plan is not for you to be poor but rich. We aren't just ambassadors *of* the wealth of God; we are ambassadors *with* the wealth of God! We are producers and distributors on a mission to destroy the works of the devil, and poverty is one of the devil's most destructive works.

This has been a controversial topic in and outside of the body of Christ. There are some believers whose focus is primarily on the spiritual benefits of salvation. They love God, they win souls, they are faithful believers, and they contribute positively to their communities. On the other hand, many Christians have received a revelation from the Book of Deuteronomy:

> But thou shalt remember the LORD thy God: for it is he that giveth thee power to get wealth, that he may establish his covenant which he sware unto thy fathers, as it is this day.
>
> —DEUTERONOMY 8:18

As businesspeople and entrepreneurs, they are creating wealth to glorify God as a testimony of God's goodness and to finance the expansion of the kingdom. Both groups are saved and going to heaven. God gives His children freedom to use their faith as they see fit. Romans 14 clearly illustrates that believers don't all believe the same! We're not to judge one another, because eventually, as Romans 14:12 says, "Every one of us shall give account of himself to God."

I believe that many poor people remain poor for two reasons. There is an absence of self-production in their lives, and they've never heard the full gospel, which destroys the image that lack of wealth has produced. Consider the words of Jesus:

> Then Jesus answering said unto them, Go your way, and tell John what things ye have seen and heard; how that the blind see, the lame walk, the lepers are cleansed, the deaf hear, the dead are raised, *to the poor the gospel is preached.*
>
> —LUKE 7:22, EMPHASIS ADDED

The gospel was preached to destroy the image that lack and poverty has produced. "For as he thinketh in his heart, so is he" (Prov. 23:7).

God gives us wealth to create platforms of credibility so the world will desire to know Him. As people visited our church, we could see God building these platforms of credibility for His kingdom. When people see how well God takes care of His children, of course they want to join His family!

Affluence always leads to influence. Nowhere in the Bible does it say a poor man is powerful and mighty for the kingdom. No way. You may ask, "What about the widow who gave the two mites?" My answer is, she was following the covenant principle of God, sowing seed to break the power of lack. She was accessing her portion out of the reservoir of God.

Ecclesiastes 9:16 says, "The poor man's wisdom is despised, and his words are not heard." If you are poor, it's hard to get people to listen to you. Your influence is limited. The church was not created to be powerless and pitiful. It was created to be the wealthiest, most influential institution in the earth—and it will be before Jesus returns!

Proverbs 3:16 says wealth follows wisdom: "In her left hand are riches and honor" (NIV). If the poor man is so wise, why is he still poor? This is the same wisdom that created the universe, and it is available to us!

I like to say it this way: without the wealth, people could question your royalty. As I mentioned previously, generally there is no such thing as a poor king or queen. God told the Israelites, "I will bring you into a wealthy place" (See Psalm 66:12), and He will do the same for us. To ignore this is like having money in a bank that you don't acknowledge. I heard a story about a woman who lived on Skid Row, where hundreds of impoverished and homeless people live. She died of malnutrition, but later it was discovered that she had plenty of money hidden in a mattress and in the walls of her apartment. How sad! She obviously had the wrong self-image, one rooted in poverty rather than the abundance that Jesus died to provide for her (John 10:10).

In the Book of Psalms the Bible says, "The LORD shall increase you more and more, you and your children" (Ps. 115:14) and "Let them shout for joy...that favour my righteous cause: yea, let them say continually, Let the LORD be magnified, which hath pleasure in the prosperity of his servant" (Ps. 35:27). Your prosperity brings God pleasure and honor. It shows the world how good your heavenly Father really is!

Amen to that!

Is There No King in You?

T. L. Osborn said, "We are what God is in us." We've seen that Micah 4:9 says, "Now why dost thou cry out aloud? is there no king in thee?" And we read in 1 John 4:17, "As he is, so are we in this world." If God is in you, then He desires to live through you. And if He is to live through you, you must see yourself as He sees you. If you don't see yourself as He sees you, He doesn't express Himself through you.

God is in you now, and if He is expressing Himself through you, poverty, failure, want, a lack of success, and feeling unfulfilled will be more and more uncommon. These are the symptoms of unrighteousness, which I define as not living up to your God-given potential. With God expressing Himself through you, there's no way you could not be comfortable financially. Constantly struggling in life is a result of a lack of awareness of God in you, which means He is not being expressed through you. He calls His expression through you the "glory" (Gen. 31:1).

When you and God function as one, work becomes worship—it becomes a way the expression of God through us brings forth much fruit in the form of ideas, concepts, and insights, because He is *the* Creator.

Galatians 2:20 says, "I am crucified with Christ: nevertheless I live; yet not I, but Christ liveth in me: and the life which I now live in the flesh I live by the faith of the Son of God, who loved me, and gave himself for me." The more I die, the more God lives through me. I die to selfishness, to criticism, and even to honor from others because I know that for Him to live in me, I have to die.

The apostle Paul said, "I die daily" (1 Cor. 15:31). We must do the same.

Colossians 1 says the mystery that remained hidden from ages and generations is now manifest in God's family, and that mystery is "Christ in you, the hope of glory" (v. 27). How did such a glorious destiny for God's own offspring, His kingdom citizens, morph into such low expectations for enjoying the blessings God pronounced upon Abraham and his seed, which not only is Christ but also includes you and me?

T. L. Osborn shares some illuminating truths in his book *The Best of Life.*

> Kingdom means "realm" or "reign" or "domain." Wherever God reigns, no other power can dominate. Jesus came preaching the reign or dominion of God in people's lives. Mk 1:14.
>
> Nothing could stand before Jesus. Sickness, weakness, leprosy, impossibilities, even death yielded when Jesus Christ came to a life.
>
> He was called *Emmanuel,* which means *God with us.* Mat 1:23.[1]

No wonder Jesus says in Mark 10:27, "With men it is impossible, but not with God: for *with God* all things are possible" (emphasis added). It's time for us to turn all impossibilities into possibilities. The glory is God shining through you. Nothing is too hard for God, and as Osborn further expounded, "Nothing is too good for you."[2]

In Numbers 13, ten of the twelve men who went to spy out the land of Canaan said, "We be not able to go up against the people; for they are stronger than we" (v. 31). God could not move Israel, newly freed from Egyptian slavery, into the land of milk and honey without their desire. The principle of desire is key to breaking free of the old image. The twelve spies brought back the fruit of the land and shared with the congregation the fruit of the land that God desired them to have. However, the Israelites preferred to go back to Egypt. (Exodus 6:9 says that the cruel bondage of slavery caused them to experience "anguish of spirit.") I believe that after four hundred years of slavery, this anguish of spirit distorted their identity as the seed of Abraham who carried the blessing of Abraham. So they didn't listen to Moses, the man God chose to deliver them. That's why I say that for us to prosper, we must destroy the image that lack of wealth has produced. If the image is still there, you will want to return to Egypt, a place where you have no real control over your own destiny.

The Scriptures tell us that "the desire of the righteous shall be granted" (Prov. 10:24) and "what things soever ye desire, when ye pray, believe that ye receive them, and ye shall have them" (Mark 11:24). Satan comes to affect our desire. It is normal for our flesh to desire the physical and material provisions that God created for us here on earth. Our desire is not just for water and air but for the comforts of life! We see the principle of desire at work when migrants come to the borders of the United States. There is something deep within every person that longs for what God has provided, things spiritual *and* natural. Jesus died for us to have both.

Why has poverty (or not desiring anything more than

just enough to get by) over the centuries since the Bible was written taken such a highly esteemed place within many sectors of the church? It is because of the influence of sources outside of God's revealed will as stated in the Bible.

T. L. Osborn again sheds light on this:

> One of the cardinal doctrines of Hinduism is to *suppress all desire for any blessing, or status, or happiness, or success in life.* It teaches that we are the product of fate; that whatever state we are in, *we are to accept it with resignation.*
>
> Buddha taught that human persons could achieve a level of mental control where *all desires in life would be neutralized* and that the *very root of desire would die.* He called this "Nirvana" or *desirelessness.*
>
> But the very *yearning* for the state of *desirelessness* is in itself *DESIRE.* In fact, it is so intense that one may spend a lifetime *struggling* in desperate mental *search* of achieving this *paradise of neutrality.* It is like trying to cure a headache by getting rid of the head.
>
> *We are created with desire.*[3]

These and other influences create a mental "wall" or barrier around the mind that keeps people trapped in an image that lack is their true and ultimate destiny. They are unable to see that there is so much more available to them in life, and the first step to prospering in God is to simply believe His Word. "For what if some did not believe? shall their unbelief make the faith of God without effect? God forbid: yea, let God be true, but every man a liar" (Rom. 3:3–4).

JETS AND AIRPLANES

As God awakened my mind to the reality of His wealth and royal kingdom, He expanded my horizons beyond what I expected. One time I was invited to preach in Savannah, Georgia, and I asked, "Lord, should I take this engagement?" He said to take it. While I was there, I met a member of that church who was a high-ranking executive at Gulfstream, which makes corporate jets. They call Gulfstream jets the Cadillacs of the air. He invited me on a tour of the plant so I could see how they made these jets. That visit inspired me to even higher aspirations of excellence in every area of my life.

When I got back to Chicago, the man called to ask how I had enjoyed my visit to his Gulfstream plant.

"It was an eye-opener," I told him. Then I asked a question that had been on my mind. "Who buys your Gulfstream jets?"

"Wealthy people—like the royal family in Saudi Arabia, for example," he said. "They buy them a couple at a time and give one to friends when they visit."

Again, an actual royal family was demonstrating the kingdom lifestyle more than most Christians do. God was putting before my eyes examples of these lifestyles to provoke me to royal ambitions. God has made every child of His household rich beyond our wildest imaginations. We are the seed of Abraham, the father of faith. The blessing of Abraham includes an empowerment for financial prosperity. Abraham was so wealthy that he literally had his own trained army that defeated kings! We are blessed just as faithful Abraham was blessed (Gal. 3:9). Whatever God did for him, He has promised to do for us. Our royalty distinguishes us and creates a clear difference between us and the rest of the world, as it did for Abraham: "The LORD has blessed my master [Abraham] greatly, and he has become great" (Gen. 24:35, NKJV).

When we live in the full revelation of who we are, including financially, we become wealthier than we might have dreamed. Scarcity is a state of mind, a manner of thinking. Jesus said, "If you believe, you will see the glory of God." (See John 11:40.)

I remember a guest minister telling a church I was visiting, "Everybody in here can have an airplane." He heard the people sigh in unbelief, so he said, "Let me ask you this. Does everybody in here have a car?" Most people nodded.

Then he said, "If you can have a car, why can't you have an airplane?"

Someone responded, "Because we don't need an airplane."

He said, "You don't need a car. You could get a ride every day or catch public transportation."

His point was that the enemy takes over people's minds and causes us to think that some things are too lavish or too expensive for us to have. We get into this mindset that says, "Too much wealth and nice things promote avarice or opulence." But in God's way of thinking, it's not enough! God wants you to live on His level. Some people think that a Rolls-Royce is more valuable than they are, so they never see themselves owning one. The truth is that we are far more valuable than an automobile or an airplane. No amount of money could redeem us from sin and death. God had to give the life of His only begotten Son, Jesus. That is a dramatic statement of how valuable your life is.

God said in Isaiah 55:8, "For my thoughts are not your thoughts, neither are your ways my ways, saith the LORD." As I've mentioned, the Bible promises, "As he [a man] thinketh in his heart, so is he" (Prov. 23:7). We have to allow God to pull up our level of thinking, as He was doing with me and with our congregation in our new location. Even Jesus' first miracle in the Bible was a miracle of luxury (turning water into fine wine). God has the very best set aside for us. It is time for the church to move from the place of scarcity and "just enough" into our promised land of more than enough.

A WEALTHY CHURCH

Again, the church should be the wealthiest institution, and God's people should be the wealthiest people, on the face of the earth. Our lifestyles should stagger the imagination of the world. Why? Because we have a larger responsibility than any other people to evangelize the world and complete the assignment God gave to Adam in the Book of Genesis. Jesus said, "Let your light so shine before men, that they may see your good works [I call them staggering works], and glorify your Father which is in heaven" (Matt. 5:16).

The church is responsible for fulfilling in the nations the prophecy that was spoken in Ezekiel 36:35: "This land that was desolate is become like the garden of

Eden; and the waste and desolate and ruined cities are become fenced, and are inhabited." Without ample financial resources, millions of souls could be lost for the kingdom of God. Wealth is not about having a bunch of "stuff." Wealth is given to fund our royal assignments to win the world to Jesus. It is also given to display the character of our Father God and show how kind and generous He is to all of His children.

The world is desperately looking for the manifestation of the sons of God. They want to see the kingdom on display. They hunger for a revelation of their royalty that makes sense of their lives. The remedies and solutions of this world are far from enough. The wisdom and intelligence of Egypt could not deliver Egypt from famine. They needed Joseph, because the blessing of the Lord was on Joseph's life. The world now needs you, because you are a royal son or daughter with supernatural solutions. They don't need the world system's so-called solutions anymore. The world system is bankrupt, full of empty promises and enslavement. It leads people into financial slavery with principles of dependency and debt. The world offers mortgages; our King offers more than enough. The world offers welfare, but our King offers wealth-fare! We belong to a different government with a royal (and debt-free) standard. Our government provides a new economy of wealth, a new destiny, and a superior King who does not enslave His children with money.

These promises are yours right now. They can never be greater than at this very moment. God did not say, "I will make you rich in the future." Accepting Jesus puts you in the wealthiest family in the universe and gives you access to all the financial wealth and blessings God has prepared on the earth, for you are His heir. In accepting Jesus, you become part of the richest family ever known to mankind, regardless of where you are, where you were born, your color, or your background. You have free access into the financial reservoirs of God.

God's promises are present tense, right now. He's not going to make you strong in the sweet by-and-by. He said, "Let the weak say, I am strong" (Joel 3:10). Get ahold of the "I Am" reality of God. He is not "I'm going to be" or "I used to be." Nothing in the Bible says, "You are going to be healed." It says, "By His stripes you are healed." (See Isaiah 53:5.) Healing is a part of your inheritance, and so is being rich. How do you get healed? You legislate it with your words of faith. How do you get rich? You legislate it with your words of faith and the kingdom principle of sowing and reaping. You start declaring, "By His stripes I am healed!" "Wealth and riches are in my house." Declare God's royal promises in your life now!

God wants us to reign on the earth. He's training us to be a walking distribution center of wealth and provision. In Matthew chapter 2, the wise men came to the house of the king Jesus and brought gifts of gold and spices. Some estimate their gifts were worth almost $400 million. That's what you bring to a King! The question is, Can we receive that kind of financial inheritance? Are we ready to accept and steward kingdom resources?

I faced that test when God told me to buy the biggest piece of property our ministry had ever purchased.

BUYING THE SHOPPING MALL

After our church outgrew the office building in Forest Park, we started holding our services at the Chez Roue banquet hall. We rented the hall twice a week, on Wednesdays and Sundays, and every week the ministry team packed up all of our equipment—sound system, chairs, and other materials—and moved it in and out of the facility. We even had to rent the moving trucks. It was a lot of work setting up, tearing down, and cleaning up the messes from late-night dances that took place there on Saturday nights. But the ministry volunteers were faithful in their service and excited to serve as they saw God increase the ministry more and more.

Then one Sunday after our last service, I came out of the front door of the banquet hall and looked across the street at a thirty-three-acre, almost-vacant shopping mall that had been in decline for several years. As I looked at it, the Lord spoke clearly to my heart: "Buy that shopping mall."

Guess how this man of faith responded to God's command?

I thought, "Why? What on earth am I going to do with a mall?"

My faith was indeed being stretched! The mall was huge, much larger than anything I could see myself believing for. I knew that it was not officially for sale and had passed through the hands of two owners who were unsuccessful in turning it around. I had a number of excuses ready to try to tear down the command of God. And boy, I went to work on it. You see, the enemy has cleverly programmed God's people to desire leftovers and little things rather than big, lavish, excellent things. We so easily forget that the assignments God gives us will always be bigger than what we can accomplish in our own strength. Why? He wants to be our only Source. When God is all you need, you have access to all of heaven's resources.

We don't have heaven's permission to say, "I don't have the money to do that," or, "That vision is too big for us to accomplish." Our provision has been laid up for us in heaven. How can we deny that it is there? God knew what we needed to complete our kingdom assignments before we even knew there was a kingdom! He has already provided for us, materially and in every other way. As the scripture says, "What soldier has to pay his own expenses?" (1 Cor. 9:7, NLT). Not one.

To buy the mall, God gave me a seed from the Word of God to meditate on. It was Joshua 1:3: "Every place that the sole of your foot shall tread upon, that have I given unto you." As I began meditating on this, my capacity to receive expanded, and I received understanding of how to do what God was asking me to do. My faith began to grow. I held tightly to that verse when my mind was bombarded by doubt and excuses for not buying the property. The only thing the enemy can't stop is faith. Faith connects you to God's ability. I was like a dog on a bone concerning the promise in that verse, and I repeated Joshua 1:3 over and over so that my faith could come by hearing the Word of God spoken by my own mouth (Rom. 10:17).

Then the Lord led our ministry to sow a financial seed. When we did, miracles began to happen. We experienced favor with the sellers, and they dropped the asking price down to something unheard of, and we purchased the mall for several million dollars less than the sellers initially proposed. I'm almost tempted to say—and I mean this in a good way—"We got it at a steal." But it was God's correct price for everyone involved.

Our season at the Chez Roue banquet hall ended as we took ownership of the shopping mall!

Each time the ministry moved to a larger place, the kind of people coming to our church changed, and they became a little more educated and prosperous. This produced a pleasing mixture of people from all backgrounds; as the Bible says, "The rich and poor meet together" (Prov. 22:2). No matter where someone is financially, the Holy Spirit tutors all of us from a slave mentality to a royal mentality. We were receiving this revelation together, everyone at his or her own level and pace.

God also changed my thinking. He showed me how the kingdom grows and expands, just like our church was doing. He demonstrated the power of influence and affluence and the operation of royalty in the life and finances of a ministry that submitted to the orders of the King.

He was using us to create kingdom environments like I had in Tuskegee, where other people would realize they were Superman (or Superwoman) too.

CHAPTER 11

CREATING ROYAL ENVIRONMENTS

❖────────────────❖

GOD DIDN'T PUT Adam in the Garden of Eden for him to stay there. It was the starting line, not the finish line. Adam's domain was the entire globe. Everywhere he went, he was assigned to create Garden of Eden environments. This is still humanity's assignment on the earth. It has been restored to us by Jesus Christ, who reconciled us to the Father and to our original purpose.

As our church grew in size and scope and moved into locations that accommodated bigger congregations and greater ministry, it created royal environments like the one I had experienced growing up in Tuskegee. My upbringing and exposure to greatness at an early age gave me a vision of life and the world like Booker T. Washington's, if I chose to put it to use. Washington didn't just create activity with no results. His work, and now legacy, impacted the world. He was able to show people that they were not consumers but producers. Not beggars but owners. Not borrowers but lenders.

Visionaries challenge those around them to see themselves and the world with new eyes, from a higher level of sight. Washington did this by challenging and changing the presumed destiny of millions of uneducated and disenfranchised ex-slaves with the prophet Micah's question, "Why dost thou cry out aloud? is there no king in thee?" (4:9). Washington proved the answer was yes, there was.

KINGS RULE BY VISION

Vision is the most powerful thing on the earth aside from the Holy Spirit, because vision is the operation of faith. Faith is not blind, as the old saying goes. It is seeing something that others cannot. Faith is a type of inner vision that gives you the power to persevere through challenging circumstances. Vision is the hope that causes acceleration toward the goal you're aiming for. It makes you unstoppable.

But so many people live without clear vision for their lives. Proverbs 29:18 says, "Where there is no vision, the people perish." The Amplified Bible, Classic Edition calls vision "redemptive revelation of God," and the ESV translates *perish* as "cast off restraint." Another translation says, colorfully, the people "run wild" when vision is absent (NLT). Let me put it in my terms: "Without a revelation of royalty, people end up perishing because they cast off restraint and run wild." Such is the power of vision.

Vision flows from our revelation of royalty. Royalty gives us eyes to see what God shows us; vision is the substance of what we see. Vision is a clear picture of conditions that do not currently exist—a strong mental image of the future. Dr. Martin Luther King Jr. had vision, and it started a movement that changed a nation. Vision is a snapshot of your destiny and an accurate indicator of what your life will become. What you envisioned yesterday, good or bad, has become a reality in your life today. What you envision today will write your future—so it is critical to get God's vision for your life as soon as possible.

I learned the importance of vision in the military while flying fighter jets, where having proper vision literally meant life or death. My training in the US Air Force included how to use the plane's radar system to zero in on a certain target. While I was flying, my radar screen gave me the ability to "see" more than two hundred miles in front of me, picking up dozens of airplanes that appeared as tiny dots or blips on my radar screen. This allowed me to anticipate and strategize for the situation I was flying into. Flying into enemy territory without radar would have been foolhardy and gotten my squadron killed.

Like the radar screen in my fighter jet, when "the eyes of your understanding [are] enlightened" (Eph. 1:18), you can see what is in the distance. You can anticipate obstacles, avoid enemies, and zero in on your target in advance, because you see by faith before you even get there.

ROYAL ENVIRONMENTS IMPART KINGLY VISION

Royal environments are designed to give people not only a revelation of their royalty but a vision of their royal future to go along with it. I saw this operate firsthand when I was a manager at IBM.

While I was employed there, IBM underwent a reorganization and twice moved me as a manager to different locations to lead different sales teams. Both of these relocations put me at the bottom of the heap, so to speak, because when you are the newest manager, you seem to get the worst people—the ones who sleep late, work less, and want to leave early. The people assigned to me presented a challenge to motivate, but a manager's duty is to train others. I concluded they did not offer much value because they did not have much vision. Giving them vision became my entire goal because I believed their performance would take care of itself once vision was in place.

One young man was new to IBM and was assigned to me to manage. His father was a well-known lawyer in downtown Chicago, but this kid had some kinks that needed to be worked out. I gave him a physical territory reaching into Indiana—a good territory with potential. Yet after a month he asked to talk to me.

"Bill, there's nothing in my territory," he whined. "There's no potential there in computer sales."

"Come on," I said.

He continued, "I think I've been given a raw deal here."

I didn't chastise him or degrade him. Rather, I said, "I will go out with you twice a week for six weeks, and we'll see what's out there." He seemed surprised by my offer, but that is exactly what we did.

At the end of the year, this young man was among the top salesmen in our region. He wrote a letter expressing his thankfulness that I would lead him by example. All I had done was given him a new set of eyes for a while—my eyes. We didn't do anything different, and I didn't teach him some dynamic selling technique. I just let him borrow my vision for a while until it became his own.

An African American woman was assigned to me on the systems side at IBM. Nobody wanted her to work for them, but I thought she had potential. I really didn't do anything special except to create an environment of vision where she could see herself differently. After a year or so, everybody wanted her to work for them. Her potential was being realized. She had a royal vision of herself serving at a high level in the company.

Another woman who worked for me was kind of mean. She had been in an accident and had a leg amputated. She was assigned to me, and I found her to be as smart as a whip but hard to deal with as a person. Again, I can't say I did much except to allow my revelation of royalty to create an environment that helped change her vision of herself. By the end of the year, everybody wanted to work with her. She was acting queenly instead of quarrelsome.

The awards we received as a team and individually had less to do with planning and strategy and more to do with creating environments where people latched on to a positive vision for their lives and careers. My employees moved into a revelation of their royalty and purpose. They saw themselves differently and had a much better experience of life. Vision had shown them their value, and they pursued it wholeheartedly, with much success.

YOUR ROYAL IDENTITY WILL TAKE YOU IN THE DIRECTION OF YOUR THOUGHTS

God said, "For my thoughts are not your thoughts, neither are your ways my ways" (Isa. 55:8). Notice that your
ways follow your thoughts. Think about that for a minute.
All you and I need to do to change our direction is to
change our thinking. You will always move in the direction of your most dominant thoughts.

People who struggle, such as those I described at IBM,
are those who have not been taught to have vision. They
don't know how to apply God's principle of seeing it
before they get it. When your thinking changes, it moves
you almost without your knowing it. Vision has this mag-
netic, invisible pull that redirects our entire lives. It can
apply to any area of our lives and any problem.

For example, I learned over time that if my vision is to
make down payments when buying something new, then I
will make down payments on everything. But if my vision
is to pay cash and remain debt-free, I will pay cash for
things and remain debt-free. I used to make down payments on everything, but now I pay cash for everything,
including our house and our cars. Our finances didn't
really change, but our vision for how to use our money did.

Your outcome depends on how you see things. Jesus
never saw lack, sickness, death, or calamity. He saw
only solutions. He always knew what He would do—
He had vision for every circumstance. We never read
where Jesus became fearful or flustered about anything.
Why? Because Jesus received direction from His Father,
not from earthly circumstances. When He had to feed
thousands of people in a desert place, He simply told the

disciples to make the people sit down. Then, holding two small fish and five loaves of bread, Jesus gave thanks. The disciples distributed the food until everyone was full. (See John 6.)

Jesus saw the multitude fed (vision). Then He walked it out in the natural.

When Jesus arrived at the home of Lazarus and was told he had been dead four days, Jesus simply prayed and said, "Lazarus, come forth" (John 11:43).

Jesus saw Lazarus raised from the dead before He raised him from the dead.

Jesus saw blind eyes opened and the lame walking. What Jesus saw, He said. And like His Father, what Jesus said always manifested! Jesus taught this principle in the Book of Mark:

> For verily I say unto you, That whosoever shall say unto this mountain, Be thou removed, and be thou cast into the sea; and shall not doubt in his heart, but shall believe that those things which he saith shall come to pass; he shall have whatsoever he saith.
>
> —MARK 11:23

One man of God said, "You cannot boldly say what you have never seen." Jesus could boldly say, "Be healed," because He had vision for the person to be healed. He would say, "Peace, be still" (Mark 4:39), because Jesus saw the peace in advance.

I remember putting this principle into practice back when I first got saved. I used to listen to a Bible teacher on the radio who told of how he laid his bills on the kitchen table and spoke to them, saying, "Debts, I'm talking to you, and I command you to be paid off, dematerialize, and disappear, in the name of Jesus." He said in that same year, his debts were completely reduced to zero—supernaturally! That inspired me, and God is no respecter of persons, so I did the same thing. I commanded my bills to be paid off, in Jesus' name, and continued to follow God's directions on my sowing. From that year onward Veronica and I purposed personally to owe no man or woman anything but to love them, and that was more than thirty years ago. I had the vision to do it!

JOSEPH BUSINESS SCHOOL

One of the callings God gave me recently was to start a business school that would compete at the highest level with Ivy League business schools. We named it the Joseph Business School because Joseph got a glimpse of his royalty when his father put the coat of many colors on him. That coat, a symbol of a king's anointing, had to do with a revelation of royalty and its many colors with the many nations Joseph would save from the famine with that anointing. In the same way, we want our school to function as a "Joseph" by serving many nations and training people to raise up a new and royal economy—one that will not fail or go through cycles of depression. If an economy is based on God's principles, it cannot fail. What is needed are vision and revelation to make it happen.

God instructed us to run the school like an entrepreneurship center that teaches students how to build businesses God's way. These businesses are designed to prosper even in tough times because they are based on God's kingdom economy, not the world's. Though our faculty are well-educated—with advanced degrees from Wellesley, Harvard, Wharton, and Stanford—our target students are those who may not have access to higher education or the top business schools but desire to learn and start successful businesses that will change the economies of their communities, cities, and nations. Here is where vision can make the most difference. For them, vision acts like rocket fuel, propelling them into the stratosphere of their actualized potential.

The seed for JBS actually started years earlier when I started the Partners Program for African American young men. We recruited our first group of twenty students from the junior high and high schools of Chicago Public Schools. Most had no vision beyond being the next great athlete, because that was the only level of vision they had been exposed to. Few had met a lawyer, doctor, or other professional in everyday life. During the program, we took the youth to places around Chicago they had never been to see things they had never seen. One such place was O'Hare International Airport. As normal as it is for many of us to travel to an airport, it was an eye-opener for them. We also took them to the commodities exchange and other vision-expanding places.

We hosted people in our classroom who had succeeded in a variety of fields to give the youth a vision for the kind of people they could be. At the end of one class, we had the students draw what they wanted to be. One student drew a picture we couldn't quite figure out, so we asked him, "What is that?"

"One of my hotels," he said.

Now, that's thinking like a king!

The Joseph Business School, through its R.I.S.E. prison ministry, is even planting visionary environments in correctional facilities like Chicago's Cook County Jail. The program teaches business and leadership classes, financial literacy, reading and writing, and Bible classes all behind the walls. Our program has proved so valuable that companies sent representatives to the first-ever job fair inside the jail, which resulted in inmates having jobs waiting for them in the community after their release.

JBS is impacting the world with partnership locations on five continents and an online program. We also started an executive accelerator program for people with established businesses who want to scale up their companies or go global by applying kingdom principles.

As citizens of the kingdom of God, we are not here to compete but to dominate. We intend to change the world through this school. How? By releasing value by way of vision and God's anointing to do exploits. Just as I helped unlock people's talent and energy at IBM, our business school is doing the same by casting vision and offering practical training as well. We believe the Holy Spirit can take anyone from any level to a much higher place. If you can see something different, you can do something different.

That's vision!

PROTECTING VISION

At a ministers' meeting I attended, a man of God prophesied to me regarding something I had been believing God for. Then he said, "Don't let the devil steal it." Those words really struck me.

I had seen such a thing happen in my own beloved Tuskegee. A leader rose up with a different kind of vision, not in the vein of Booker T. Washington's vision. This vision was much inferior. As a result, Tuskegee declined and has never recovered its high position. Someone "stole" Tuskegee's vision. The environment of royalty no longer exists there, though I am believing that one day it will be restored.

Protect the vision God gives you. Shield it from harm, erosion, doubt, subversion, and attack. What God has given you to do may be unlike anything that has ever been done before. That doesn't matter. We cannot allow vision stealers to take what God has given us. Value your vision, guard it, and don't be so quick to tell everyone about it. Telling your vision to the wrong people can be perilous. Just ask Joseph! People without a vision may discourage you because they cannot see what you see. Intentionally put yourself around leaders, and you will find people who will applaud your vision.

Beware of mental clutter as well. When we allow cable news or social media to fill our minds with extraneous information, it can be extremely difficult to focus and bring forth in the earth what God has revealed to us. When a thought gets in my mind that saps or obstructs my vision, I do like I did in the cockpit of my fighter jet way back when I was a pilot. On our radar screens we could put our pointer on one particular target and squeeze the radar trigger. When you did that, every other blip on your screen would instantly disappear. Only the targeted dot remained in sight. I compare this to focusing on the Word of God until every negative thought and word of unbelief disappears from the screen of your mind. Choose the thought you want to focus on, "squeeze the trigger," and let all other thoughts disappear.

Abraham did this. "And being not weak in faith, he considered not his own body now dead, when he was about an hundred years old, neither yet the deadness of Sarah's womb: he staggered not at the promise of God through unbelief; but was strong in faith, giving glory to God" (Rom. 4:19–20).

It says he "considered not," meaning Abraham didn't focus on the negative. He protected his vision from threats.

I can tell you after decades of walking with God in many different environments, vision is what gets me up in the morning. Our ministry now has two shopping malls, a congregation of thousands, and a television broadcast. I also have a wonderful wife, three terrific children, and eight grandchildren for whom I am a role model and leader. My vision is important for them as well as me.

Everywhere you go, create environments where royalty and vision can flourish. Then you will be doing your part to restore planet Earth to the paradise God intended it to be.

CHAPTER 12

SURPRISING EFFECTS OF YOUR ROYAL IDENTITY

✦———————————✦

T HE REVELATION OF royalty has many positive side effects. I consider them to be part of its purpose, but some of these effects may surprise you. Let me share several of the unexpected things your royal identity will accomplish in your life.

YOUR ROYAL IDENTITY WILL RECONCILE

Back when I was training to fly fighter jets, I was the only African American in our class. There were nearly fifty of us living and learning together. Naturally, it never occurred to me that I was different from anyone else just because I was another color. I had my royal revelation from Tuskegee, and I was happy to be there, shoulder-to-shoulder with everyone else.

My roommate and I lived together in officers' quarters and bunked in a two-bedroom apartment. The place also had a kitchenette and a living room. As graduation approached, his family came to visit. I was in the bedroom taking a nap the afternoon before ceremonies when I woke up to the sound of people talking loudly in the living room.

"You mean all this time you've been bunking with a Black man [actually, he used the more derogatory phrase]?" my roommate's father's voice boomed. "They let you bunk with him?"

His prejudice caught me by surprise, but it did not hurt my feelings or erode my image. I just thought how strange it was that someone would put a box around his thinking that way. I could have gotten angry and made an issue of the racist remarks with my roommate or even with our superiors, but it was as if the insult never landed on me. Royalty decides what it will allow and what it will not allow. Someone else's racism was his or her problem. It could twist the person's thinking, but it didn't need to twist mine. My roommate and I graduated the next day and became pilots.

A few years later I was in Southeast Asia serving as a fighter pilot in the Vietnam War. One night my direct supervisor had too much to drink. He came into the control center where I was working and announced, "I hate Negroes."

This man had been passed over twice for promotions and had become embittered. He was from the South, and though segregation had officially ended, the mindset held on. Angrily he railed about Black people in my presence for a while. But it didn't affect my image. His words couldn't touch my identity because my identity was rooted too deep in me.

"Boss, don't feel that way. We're not hurting you," I

said. My response was one of mercy and genuine concern for him. I knew that with these kinds of attitudes and habits, he wouldn't be allowed to stay long in the military. Anyway, it was no use arguing with a drunk man speaking out of his pain, and I felt a lot better "turning the other cheek" as Jesus said, though I wasn't a Christian at the time.

My role model, Booker T. Washington, responded to racism the same way, which is why he kept growing in authority. By this time, I too had learned how to process other people's prejudices almost better than they did, and what could have erupted into a forest fire I was able to extinguish. I did not report my boss to his superiors, but over time I heard he had lost his military career for reasons I never knew.

Second Corinthians 5:18 says, "And all things are of God, who hath reconciled us to himself by Jesus Christ, and hath given to us the ministry of reconciliation." Royalty reconciles when it can. Sometimes this simply means avoiding needless offense and conflict. You can't always change people's hearts and minds, but you can respond in a reconciling way that refuses to let racism define the conversation or environment. Only a revelation of royalty can empower you to do that.

YOUR ROYAL IDENTITY WILL DRIVE OUT THE SLAVE MENTALITY

Every community has its problems—Black, White, and every other color. But I was still surprised to find negative mindsets in the Black communities I encountered outside of Tuskegee.

When I became a pilot, my habit was to go to the local high school and set up a day to bring students in for a field trip. Why? Because that's what had been done with us in Tuskegee. They took us to interesting places to give us vision for our future, and it seemed normal to help create those environments for others wherever I went.

But many in the Black communities at military bases and later in business possessed remnants of another mentality. This was aimed at getting handouts, freebies, preferential promotion, and so forth. It was a narrative that put institutions and corporations in control and made Black people the beggars. That didn't feel natural to me at all. In my city, the Black community had helped the White community! They needed us as much as or more than we needed them. We were intellectually and economically on par with each other. Nothing could erase that reality from my mind. It was in me for good.

So it distressed me to meet qualified, perfectly capable minorities who felt they had been selected to fill the minority quota and meet a company's or branch's racial objectives. People with this mentality, no matter how talented they were, adopted a mindset of just getting by, doing what the powers that be asked them to do. I had a different vision altogether. I didn't want a handout or unearned promotion—I wanted to be the president of a division, maybe even the chairman of the company one day, based on my performance. My inner image showed. One time during my corporate career, my boss even sent me to the airport to pick up the president of one of the divisions of IBM, which I recognized as an informal get-to-know-you interview for me as they vetted potential leaders within the company.

Anyone, Black or White, can have a slave mentality. It says that someone else holds all the power over you. This kind of thinking is unrighteous, inferior, guilt-based, and the opposite of the revelation of royalty. When you walk in your proper identity, you will never look to others for what they can do for you. You will walk and live and behave like an owner, not a beggar. This was the journey of the prodigal son, from begging for food in a hog yard to realizing he was the heir and owner of a rich estate and had no need to beg.

No matter your race, education, or background, nobody was made to be a beggar relying on handouts and unwarranted favor. Royalty walks with its head held high. Ecclesiastes chapter 10 says, "There is an evil which I have seen under the sun....servants upon horses, and princes walking as servants upon the earth" (vv. 5, 7).

YOUR ROYAL IDENTITY WILL DEFINE YOUR DISPOSITION

Royalty has a certain disposition, a certain bearing, a kingly and queenly way about it. It projects an identity, an aura of majesty. It has the flavor of the palace and the aroma of the throne room.

A royal disposition is many things: being well able, God-fearing, truthful; rejecting covetousness; maintaining a clear, impactful vision; being loving, daring, risk-taking, joyful, unsusceptible to negative circumstances, humble, trustworthy, and much more. A royal disposition, at its foundation, simply means walking in the fruit of the Spirit, which is "love, joy, peace, longsuffering, kindness, goodness, faithfulness, gentleness, self-control" (Gal. 5:22–23, NKJV).

Having the wrong disposition can affect your promotion. When I was working at IBM years ago, my boss was planning to promote me and had invited several senior executives to watch me make a presentation. On the way to the meeting, a colleague who was African American began to share how he had suffered because of the injustices done to him by his company. I allowed his experience to affect my disposition that day to such a degree that my presentation reflected my anger. Needless to say, the meeting didn't go well, my boss was furious, and I did not get the promotion.

Thank God for His mercy and that my story didn't end there. Sometime later, God gave me another opportunity, and I disciplined myself to walk in the disposition of royalty. The results were much better, and I continued to climb higher in the company.

Daniel displayed a royal disposition when God delivered him from the lions' den:

> And when he [the king] came to the den, he cried out with a lamenting voice to Daniel. The king spoke, saying to Daniel, "Daniel, servant of the living God, has your God, whom you serve continually, been able to deliver you from the lions?" Then Daniel said to the king, "O king, live forever!"
> —DANIEL 6:20–21, NKJV

Did you see what he did? Daniel had been stuck all night in a dirty den with hungry lions, but he didn't curse the king. The Scriptures instruct us not to curse the king (Eccles. 10:20). Instead, Daniel blessed the king with the blessing of long life. As a result, Daniel was promoted, and those who conspired against him were thrown into the den and eaten by the lions. The more you look into that story, the more you will see how a royal disposition served Daniel so well. Circumstances always uncover and reveal who we really are, and Daniel came forth like pure gold.

Having a royal disposition helps manifest God's majesty and power in our lives. There are certain things that royalty won't receive, certain places that royalty won't go, and certain things that royalty won't do. There are even things royalty won't eat and drink. Yes, the Holy Spirit will tell you what and how to eat—and if you need to lose some weight! He will tell you not to watch certain television shows, read certain books, visit certain news sites, or use certain language. Remember, He is training you for reigning. Rulership is not granted to the undisciplined, the loose cannons, the low-minded, or the lazy.

Having a royal disposition means we are self-controlled and maintain a kingly bearing in all situations.

Your Royal Identity Will Test Your Ability to Receive Revelation

One day, a radio station owner in Hammond, Indiana, offered me fifteen minutes a week every Saturday morning on his station to give a short message. I had to pay for the time, but it was a very good price. I drove over to meet with him and felt the Lord say, "Take it," so I agreed to the Saturday morning time slot. I would

185

supply a fifteen-minute teaching every week and pay a certain amount to him.

When I got home, the Lord spoke to me so clearly, "What are you doing, agreeing to go on the radio once a week?"

"I'm obeying You!" I said.

"No, I want you on every weekday, Monday through Friday," the Lord said. "People need to hear about faith more than once a week."

Wow, did that strike fear into my heart! I wasn't so concerned about the greatly increased cost—five times a week versus one time, and on more expensive weekday mornings. I was mainly concerned that I would run out of things to say! I was in a place of doubt about my ability to receive revelation for the task God had given me. At that time, I didn't fully understand that when you give away what you have in obedience to God, He fills you up again. I was thinking more about saving something for tomorrow, but that's a scarcity mentality, holding on to day-old bread. Again "The Tutor" was tutoring me into royalty. God had to take me out of a shortage mindset and into overflow.

I called the radio station owner back and said, "The Lord is speaking to me about going on the air for fifteen minutes every weekday morning."

"Can you afford that?" he asked me.

I responded by faith, "Yes, the Lord is going to help me with it."

Faith in the kingdom becomes your currency, and I had the money in the form of faith. God knew that.

We hung up, and without telling me, the owner called a

mutual acquaintance and asked if we had enough money to buy that kind of airtime! She told him, "I don't know if he has enough money, but he has enough faith."

The owner took a chance on me. I set up a little recording booth at our church location and put it on my schedule to come in at 5 a.m. to record a week's worth of teachings. Then I sent them to the radio station. We were never late to pay our bills. More than that, God gave me plenty of revelation for every day's episode. As a result of that faith step many years ago, our ministry now reaches almost a billion potential households on a weekly basis by some form of media. If my scarcity mentality had won out, we might not even be on the radio. Don't despise small beginnings!

God will always give you more than enough revelation to meet the needs of every situation. One man of God said that "revelation is the greatest asset in the school of faith." That is why the psalmist wrote, "Open thou mine eyes, that I may behold wondrous things out of thy law" (Ps. 119:18). Luke 24:45 says, "Then opened he [Jesus] their understanding, that they might understand the scriptures." God never runs out of revelation, and He is always willing to share.

YOUR ROYAL IDENTITY WILL SIFT YOUR RELATIONSHIPS

Walking in revelation of your royalty can sometimes cause a strain and sifting in relationships. A good example of this is in the Book of Genesis. There, a man named Lot was blessed by his relationship with his uncle, Abraham. The Scripture says, "Abram was very rich in cattle, in silver, and in gold" (Gen. 13:2). It goes on to say that Lot, who was associated with Abraham, "had flocks, and herds, and tents" (v. 5). Notice how Lot was blessed because of his association with Abraham. He was reaping the results of a royal environment.

But when the land was no longer able to support both men's herds and possessions and Abraham's and Lot's herdsmen began to quarrel, the relationship became strained. Abraham (still named Abram at the time) said to Lot, "Let there be no strife....Is not the whole land before thee?" (Gen. 13:8–9), and Abraham let his nephew be the first to choose the land that he wanted.

Lot's eyes were drawn to the fruitful plain where the cities of Sodom and Gomorrah lay, and Lot moved in the direction of his desire, to Sodom. This move away from the royal environment (his royal association with Abraham) eventually ended in disaster for the city and for Lot's own family, though God spared him and his daughters from immediate destruction.

For his part, Abraham really did nothing wrong to cause separation in his relationship with Lot. He simply walked through life with a royal perspective. Over time this created division between them. Royal identity will always separate you from the person who is not choosing to live in his or her royal identity. That person will probably not understand the choices you make or why you make them. Ultimately the relationship will come to some kind of pause or end.

This can be a hurdle for some people who don't want to lose their family members, communities, or best friends. Relationships give a great deal of comfort and satisfaction, but they also can stand in the way of pursuing God's plans for our lives or walking in our actual identity. Abraham knew he was called to go higher. He allowed Lot to separate from him, maybe even knowing that Lot would suffer by no longer being under Abraham's royal covering of prosperity and protection. (This played out not long after, when Lot and his family were taken captive by a foreign king, only to be rescued by mighty, shrewd Abraham and his army.) There are many examples in the Bible of people who started dreaming God-given dreams, only to have those dreams separate them from family and friends. That is the price of going higher and living in our true identities.

YOUR ROYAL IDENTITY WILL MAKE OTHERS JEALOUS

Sometimes when your royal identity starts manifesting in your life, it will provoke others to full-blown jealousy. This is what happened to Joseph. In Genesis 37, Joseph dreamed about becoming a ruler and seeing his brothers bow down to him. He made the mistake of sharing the dream with his brothers and father. His brothers got so jealous that they wanted to kill him. Instead, they threw him into a pit, and he ended up being sold to Ishmaelite slave traders, who took him to Egypt and sold him as a slave.

We like to think that others will celebrate our royal calling with us, but like Joseph's brothers, even our closest family members will be tempted to jealousy. That's just the way it is, though I wish I could tell you differently. Most people become jealous and resentful and have to overcome that before they celebrate with you. Some never get there.

Don't be discouraged when your above-the-line identity draws forth negative responses from others. Jesus said, "They hated me without a cause" (John 15:25). Even Christian brethren may be envious of you and your new identity, and they may not even know why. It's because the enemy fears the revelation of royalty and the believers who operate in it. He stokes jealous thoughts in people around us.

When Veronica and I came to Chicago to start our ministry with only $200 and no place to stay, very few people cared about what we were preaching or teaching. But when our ministry began to grow and we eventually purchased a vacant thirty-three-acre shopping mall in a suburb of Chicago, and the ministry (located on the mall property) began to flourish—oh, did the haters begin to surface! It didn't matter that our vision was to bring economic prosperity to the area through jobs and tax revenue. Jealousy is blind to the good you do.

But no matter how hurtful people's words are or how badly they gossip about you, your responsibility is to walk in love. Remember, only you can relinquish your identity. Because Veronica and I stayed in a place of faith and love, we have the privilege of preaching the gospel all around the world, and that once-deserted shopping mall has created more than four hundred jobs and provides millions of dollars in tax revenue to the village and county. We held tightly to our royal identity and wouldn't let people's jealousy embitter us.

YOUR ROYAL IDENTITY WILL
REMOVE YOUR LID

We have seen before how God wants to take us higher in Him, living above the line and into the supernatural lifestyle. This often requires us to leave the familiar to move with Him into unfamiliar circumstances. Some royal children may feel obligated to stay where they were brought up or stick with a community that has been good to them. But leaving is often the only path to the next level.

Here's an observation: People seldom reach their full potential in the same place. God often has to move us to a new environment, away from family and the familiar, to reach our full potential. One test God gives us is, Will we go higher with Him? Will we allow our royal identity to remove the lids on our lives? Home may feel comfortable, but maybe He is calling you to attend a school in another state. Perhaps He is leading you there because He knows you will find the right leadership and opportunities to develop you into a world-class leader. Only He knows.

After buying Joseph as a slave, the Ishmaelites took him to Egypt and sold him to Potiphar. The only way Joseph would blossom was by "removing the lid," or transitioning from under Jacob's authority. Remember, it was Jacob, his father, who told Joseph to quit talking about his heavenly dream (Gen. 37:10). By saying this, Jacob was putting a lid on Joseph's life while it was clear that God was preparing Joseph for leadership.

YOUR ROYAL IDENTITY WILL TEST YOUR SOIL

Related to "lid lifting" (i.e., removing the lid the enemy tries to place on your potential) is the necessity of being planted in the right soil to become a visionary leader in God's household. As I said many times, God desires to move you from where you are to where you should be so that your gifts and potential can be maximized. Unfortunately, many people refuse to move.

When God transported a reluctant Joseph away from everything he knew and into Egypt, Joseph may not have known he was being planted in an environment that had the perfect circumstances to maximize his potential. Even when it's not ideal according to human standards, God knows what environment will best bring out your potential. You and I usually can't tell these things. We didn't create ourselves—God did. Even if we have some indication of what's inherent inside of us, our Maker is the only one who knows what it takes to draw out our true potential.

Joseph went to his new place in chains, but the chains didn't restrict his development or the anointing God had on his life. He was in the right soil. He never would have been a mighty ruler back home at his father's house. God had to move Joseph out of his current (tribal) environment, where everything was familiar to him, and take him to where he could bloom as a leader on the world's stage. If you have ever studied agriculture or planted a garden, you know that for a seed to open up and begin growing, it needs to experience the right conditions in the right soil. You can't plant an acorn in the sand or in dry, parched ground if you want it to grow. It has to be in the proper soil to take root and grow.

People are the same way. Some have all the right ingredients inside of them but can't flourish because they are not in the proper soil. As with an acorn, everything you will become is already inside of you—God is not adding anything anymore; He's developing what's already there. Inside every acorn seed is an oak tree. Entire trees exist within and can be produced from a single acorn; it is a self-contained unit with all of the necessary elements packaged within. This is called potential—all of that unrealized, unexposed ability, talent, power, and strength. It is just waiting to be planted in the right soil—just like you and me.

YOUR ROYAL IDENTITY IS TIMELESS

Some may say, "My time has past. I'm too old to do what God wants me to do. Let the younger generation handle it." Others might say, "I'm too young and too green. I'm not ready to be planted and flourish."

Let me assure you: Your royal identity knows no age. It is never too young or too old. It can accomplish anything at any time. The important thing is that you start. Start in faith and stay in faith. Abraham and Sarah had their son of promise, Isaac, when they were elderly and past child-bearing age. As we read before, Romans 4:19–20 says, "And being not weak in faith, he considered not his own body now dead, when he was about an hundred years old, neither yet the deadness of Sarah's womb: he staggered not at the promise of God through unbelief; but was strong in faith, giving glory to God."

Anyone can start making up for lost time right now. If you're still breathing, you can realize the royal, untapped potential inside of you. Harland Sanders, also known as the great Colonel Sanders, didn't start the world-famous Kentucky Fried Chicken until he was sixty-six years old! If he could start a chicken franchise at that age, you can surely start doing what God has placed on your heart to achieve. The saying "Age is only a number" is certainly true when you're dealing with God.

Paul told his young apprentice, Timothy, not to back away from ministry because he felt too young (1 Tim. 4:12). It reminds me of one of the speakers at our business conference, a young African American man who became a millionaire at age fourteen. His family had been on welfare ever since he was born, and he said one day he just got tired of being broke. He taught himself a few things, tapped into his potential, and started doing the only thing he knew to do: he painted rocks and sold them to his neighbors. From there he built one business after another, becoming a millionaire and the youngest person to have an office on Wall Street. At age twenty-one he received an honorary doctorate and was later named one of the most influential Black men in America by the National Urban League.[1]

Still think you're too young to pursue your God-given dreams?

Job chapter 32 says, "This is what Elihu, son of Barakel the Buzite, said: 'I'm a young man, and you are all old and experienced. That's why I kept quiet and held back from joining the discussion. I kept thinking, "Experience will tell. The longer you live, the wiser you become." But I see I was wrong—it's God's Spirit in a person, the breath of the Almighty One, that makes wise human insight possible'" (vv. 6–8, MSG).

YOUR ROYAL IDENTITY WILL WITHSTAND SHAKING

I got shaken for a few years when I first went to college. My brother was attending Howard University in Washington, DC, studying architecture, so I followed him there and majored in zoology with the idea of going to medical school afterward. By that time, my brother was a well-known senior, and Howard was infamous for its party scene, so I was invited to many parties. My studies took a nosedive for the first time in my life, and one day I received a failing grade in a class. My economics professor, Dr. Hoskins, said to me, "Mr. Winston, some of us have it, and some of us just don't." His words shocked me, and I was further rattled when the school asked me to take a semester off to consider my plans because my grades were so bad.

Calling my dad with the news was one of the hardest things I have ever done. He was a firm believer in education and had done everything he could to position us for success in that arena. Here I had failed. As disappointed as he was, Dad had a plan. He talked with the director of admissions at Tuskegee University, and I came home to complete my degree (which I switched to biology), minus all of the distractions. That was when I reconnected with my desire to fly airplanes, and I am glad to have made the transition back to my dreams. It was a good result for me.

But being shaken was hard. The only thing that allowed me to bounce back was that I was firmly convinced, even then, of my kingly image. No economics professor and no university could convince me I was "less than" or unable. When you are that rooted in your royal identity, nothing will come along that can shake you off course. It may feel choppy for a while, but that's when your royalty becomes your rudder and leads you back on course, like it did for me.

YOUR ROYAL IDENTITY WILL MAKE YOU MISSION-MINDED

When I returned to Tuskegee to attend university, my mind was made up: I was going to succeed no matter what. I had become mission-minded about my life. One way or another, I would have a successful outcome. I enrolled in the Reserve Officers' Training Corps (ROTC), which prepared me to enter the US Air Force after I graduated.

The military is a living example of mission-mindedness in the structure and organization of an aircraft carrier. In the military, of course, everything is by the book. Everyone knows his or her job; they are well trained to work together as an efficient team. Everyone on the team is mission-minded, so there is no strife or competition. This matters because in wartime, if people are not in their proper place or are not properly trained, someone could lose his or her life. Mission-mindedness is that important.

On an aircraft carrier, an "air boss" oversees everyone and ensures that each member of the team adheres to the established procedures and standards. The air boss successfully orchestrates the mission in a close environment and prepares the "effective readiness" of the team for wartime.

My specific role on the team was as a combat pilot, and I had my own unique preparation to be mindful of. One aspect of this "effective readiness" was what every pilot must consider: his fuel. Before you take off on a mission, your aircraft must be fully loaded with fuel. Your target may be four hundred miles north of where you are, and you may not be able to get there and back on one tank. You can't land to refuel. Rather, you have to refuel in the air by connecting with a refueling tanker. This is a difficult thing to do.

I can recall times when new pilots would come for me to train them to fly in a combat zone. They would sit in the front seat as the aircraft commander, and I would sit behind them in the cockpit. Although they were certified pilots and could fly, when they attempted to hook up to the refueling tanker for the first time, they would usually run into problems.

The jet fighter's center of gravity would shift easily because of its heavy weight, and it would dance back and forth under the refueling tanker. I had to show the officers how to keep the jet fighter balanced and still so it was able to hook up to the tanker and sit there for refueling. After a few times of trying, they could do it perfectly. It took a great deal of focus and mission-mindedness. I guarantee that when you are hooking up to a refueling tanker, you are thinking of nothing else.

That is how we need to be in our assignments that

flow from our royal identity. Mission-mindedness means everyone is working together, hitting established standards, focused on the right things. Our air boss is the Lord Himself, and I believe He is orchestrating something much greater than anything we have seen in the earth.

Your Royal Identity Enables You to Do Wondrous Things

Psalm 72:18 says, "Blessed be the LORD God, the God of Israel, who only doeth wondrous things." One Bible commentary describes "wondrous things" as "great wonders such as none else can match, leaving all others so far behind, that he remains the sole and only wonder worker."[2] When you know that you are a ruler, and you walk in your new royal identity, God's anointing will flow effortlessly through you to work miracles. Wondrous works happen when you partner with God to bring forth heaven's ideas and plans into the earth. If you serve in the business world, no competitor will be able to match what you do or how you do it! You will leave others far behind by dominating your industry and leading in your sphere of influence. Like Daniel, who was ten times better than all his peers, your royal identity will position you as a world changer and history maker.

When you have a consciousness of who you are in Christ, it changes you and everything around you. Jesus had a consciousness of who He was, and that identity never left Him. He knew He was a ruler, a king, a divine being clothed in a human body. He said things like, "My Father" and "ye are gods." When He said, "I and my

Father are one" (John 10:30), the religious leaders wanted to stone Him. They said, "For a good work we stone thee not; but for blasphemy; and because that thou, being a man, makest thyself God" (v. 33).

The enemy works overtime to keep you accepting and maintaining an image of being only human. He tries to design circumstances and events that reinforce human frailty, weakness, and having no control in life. The Holy Spirit, on the other hand, is busy doing just the opposite. He is always reinforcing your rulership and, as said before, tutoring you into royalty. He is on the inside of every born-again child of God, reminding him or her, "You are not merely human."

Again, Micah 4:9 says, "Now why dost thou cry out aloud? is there no king in thee?"

The answer is a resounding, "Yes, there is a king in me!"

The revelation of royalty is a powerful force for advancing the kingdom of God in the earth. These are just a few of the important effects your royal identity will have on people, situations, and your own life. Having observed them many times in my own life and in people around me, I offer them as spiritual insight and encouragement to help you stay on course as you walk in your royal identity.

CONCLUSION

I WAS ON A mission trip in India several years ago when I tried—and repeatedly failed—to make a phone call from my hotel room. No matter where I moved around the room, I couldn't get a signal on my cell phone. Finally, I went down to the hotel lobby to find out what was happening.

"Sir, we apologize for the inconvenience, but it is beyond our control," said the attendant at the front desk. "The large truck just outside the hotel is electronically sweeping the airwaves because the president of the United States is coming."

That explained it! The Indian government was preparing the environment—even the airwaves—for the president's safe arrival into the country.

That is a magnificent picture of what is happening on the planet today. The Holy Spirit is "sweeping the spiritual atmosphere" to prepare for the return of Jesus, our King. He is creating a royal environment for His coming, just as Isaiah prophesied, "Prepare the way for the Lord, make straight paths for our God." (See Isaiah 40:3; Matthew 3:3.)

How is God doing this? Through your royal decrees! Through the prayers, intercession, and spoken words of His royal children—you and me!

SPEAK INTO THE ATMOSPHERE

As we learned in this book, speaking faith-filled words is the way God created this world and the way we manage and elevate it to kingdom status today. Our goal is to help the whole world rise above the line by exercising our dominion mandate. We have the power, we have the calling, and we have the words to make it happen. Our legislative decrees resound through the heavens and earth and literally shape history.

Micah the prophet gave us a great example when he prophesied Jesus' birth:

> But thou, Bethlehem Ephratah, though thou be little among the thousands of Judah, yet out of thee shall he come forth unto me that is to be ruler in Israel; whose goings forth have been from of old, from everlasting.
>
> —MICAH 5:2

Watch how this happened: hundreds of years after Micah spoke and wrote those legislative words, a secular king made another decree that caused the prophet's words to be fulfilled:

> And it came to pass in those days, that there went out a decree from Caesar Augustus that all the world should be taxed....And all went to be taxed, every one into his own city. And Joseph also went up from Galilee, out of the city of Nazareth, into Judaea, unto the city of David, which is called

Bethlehem...to be taxed with Mary his espoused
wife, being great with child.

—LUKE 2:1, 3–5

Why did Caesar decide to tax the people? What moti-
vated his actions at that exact moment in time? They
were set in motion in the spiritual realm by Micah's
prophetic words released centuries earlier that Israel's
Messiah—the Savior of the whole world—would be
born in Bethlehem. And it happened just as the prophet
said. The word Micah released from heaven by faith prepared the way for the coming King, prompting a Roman
Caesar to make a decree that caused Micah's prophecy to
be fulfilled—right on time.

The Word of God is the all-controlling factor. It transcends time and extends throughout generations. Using
faith-filled words, we take dominion over the world,
bringing everything on this planet in line with heav-
en's government, the kingdom of God. Wherever we
are sent, we have a right and a duty to bring everything
that is out of line with heaven's government into divine
alignment, in preparation for our King. Angels are sent
as CEAs—covenant-enforcing agents—of your decree.
God's kingdom rules over all, and His angels "do his
commandments, hearkening unto the voice of his word"
(Ps. 103:20; see also verse 19).

CALLING THINGS INTO BEING

Let me give you a few closing examples of this. David,
speaking like the king he would become, made five dec-
larations about the outcome of his fight with Goliath:

> This day [number 1] the LORD will deliver you into
> my hand [number 2], and I will strike you [number
> 3] and take your head from you [number 4]. And
> this day I will give the carcasses of the camp of the
> Philistines to the birds of the air and the wild beasts
> of the earth, that all the earth may know that there
> is a God in Israel [number 5].
> —1 SAMUEL 17:46, NKJV

Every one of those five things happened because they were decreed. Years later, when the people of Israel were facing a different crisis, Mordecai helped Esther fulfill her destiny and declared her future by saying:

> If you keep quiet at a time like this, deliverance and
> relief for the Jews will arise from some other place,
> but you and your relatives will die. Who knows if
> perhaps you were made queen for just such a time
> as this?
> —ESTHER 4:14, NLT

Things happened exactly as Mordecai had decreed. As Ecclesiastes 8:4 says, "Where the word of a king is, there is power." Our words are so powerful that Scripture warns us as God's royal representatives to watch what we say:

> Suffer not thy mouth to cause thy flesh to sin; nei-
> ther say thou before the angel, that it was an error:
> wherefore should God be angry at thy voice, and
> destroy the work of thine hands?
> —ECCLESIASTES 5:6

Sometimes the royal decree is so ready to be proclaimed that it literally leaps out of your mouth, bypassing your natural mind. This happened to me a few years ago when I decreed in a church service, "We are turning jails into boarding schools." I didn't know how that would happen, and it wasn't my job to know. My responsibility was to speak what the Spirit of God told me to say—and the words burst forth with heavenly power.

Since that decree, our R.I.S.E. prison ministry was birthed, and every week the church's team has been teaching and ministering to 150 to 175 medium- and maximum-security inmates inside Chicago's Cook County Jail. Classes include English literacy (reading and writing), business and leadership, and a workshop on starting a business to create apps. As I mentioned previously, the R.I.S.E. team even hosted the jail's first-ever job fair "behind the walls," resulting in inmates being released with jobs waiting for them in the community. This is amazing stuff! It began with a decree straight from heaven.

In fact, the words "turning jails into boarding schools" are still expanding supernaturally and now changing prisons in the nation of South Africa. Trained by our team in the United States, Bill Winston Ministries Africa has started R.I.S.E. South Africa, which teaches business and literacy classes to inmates in correctional facilities across South Africa. Glory to God!

Prophetic words carry the supernatural ability to control this natural realm. God's Word has all-controlling power. Time can't weaken it, geographic borders can't contain it, and earthly governments can't stop it.

TIME TO GET IN THE FIGHT

The end-time church today is experiencing a direct assault of the enemy. Through spiritual deception and ungodly laws and policies, Satan is attempting to eradicate the Word of God from the face of the planet. Satan knows that God's Word, released in faith, has all-controlling power to cancel curses, reverse the effects of ungodly laws, and redirect the destinies of generations and nations.

The battle is at the church's door, and it is time to get in the fight—God's way. "For the weapons of our warfare are not carnal but mighty in God for pulling down strongholds" (2 Cor. 10:4, NKJV). Jesus, the first of many royal brothers and sisters, said, "He that believeth on me, the works that I do shall he do also; and greater works than these shall he do; because I go unto my Father" (John 14:12). He stilled storms, healed the maimed, raised the dead, paid off taxes, turned water into wine—all with words! Now it's our turn to do what He did—and greater things.

Isaiah 51:16 tells us, "And I have put My words in your mouth; I have covered you with the shadow of My hand, that I may plant the heavens, lay the foundations of the earth, and say to Zion, 'You are My people'" (NKJV). God expects us to "plant the heavens" by speaking things into existence according to His will, which He planned for the earth before the foundation of the world.

He promised that His Word would not return void (Isa. 55:11). In a recent Sunday service, I was impressed to decree, "We are taking back the public schools in the United States of America, in Jesus' name." I know it will happen because the words were of royal origin. They cannot fail.

It is time to ascend to our place as rulers and royalty, taking dominion over all the works of darkness. Believe that what you say will come to pass, and you shall have whatever you say, according to Mark 11:23. Your words spoken in faith release God's power to bring His promises to pass in your life and all around you.

Walk in your revelation of royalty today! Together we will legislate the future God has chosen for our lives and for this earth.

NOTES

CHAPTER 4
DECLARING YOUR ROYALTY OUT LOUD

1. *Merriam-Webster*, s.v. "decree," accessed March 30, 2021, https://www.merriam-webster.com/dictionary/decree.

CHAPTER 5
TUSKEGEE VISION

1. Blue Letter Bible, s.v. *"yaʿbēṣ"* accessed March 30, 2021, https://www.blueletterbible.org/lang/Lexicon/Lexicon.cfm?strongs=H3258&t=KJV.

CHAPTER 9
FROM INFORMATION TO REVELATION

1. William J. Federer, *George Washington Carver: His Life and Faith in His Own Words* (St. Louis: Amerisearch, Inc., 2008), 9, 18–19, 44, 61; see also Bill Federer, "Amazing Source for George Washington Carver's Ideas...the Bible," WND, July 11, 2016, https://www.wnd.com/2016/07/amazing-source-for-george-washington-carvers-ideas/; see also William J. Federer, *America's God and Country: Encyclopedia of Quotations,* rev. ed. (Coppell, TX: FAME Publishing, Inc., 1994; St. Louis: Amerisearch, Inc., 2000), 94.
2. Ben Carson, *Gifted Hands* (Grand Rapids, MI: Zondervan, 1990), 184.
3. Scott Sorokin, "Thriving in a World of 'Knowledge Half-Life,'" IDG Communications, April 5, 2019, https://www.cio.com/article/3387637/thriving-in-a-world-of-knowledge-half-life.html.
4. As quoted in Stephen R. Covey, *The 7 Habits of Highly Effective People* (New York: Free Press, 2004), 42.
5. Chuck Yeager and Leo Janos, *Yeager: An Autobiography* (New York: Bantam Books, 1985).

Chapter 10
The Wealthy Believer

1. T. L. Osborn, *The Best of Life* (Tulsa, OK: Osborn Ministries International, 2003), 116.
2. Osborn, *The Best of Life*.
3. Osborn, *The Best of Life*, 84–85, emphasis added.

Chapter 12
Surprising Effects of Your Royal Identity

1. "Want to Be a Millionaire? Farrah Gray Says Ask Yourself Three Questions," KLTV, July 28, 2006, https://www.kltv.com/story/5211646/want-to-be-a-millionaire-farrah-gray-says-ask-yourself-three-questions/; see also "Chapter 18: Dr. Farrah Gray," Chicken Soup for the Soul, accessed March 30, 2021, https://www.chickensoup.com/book-story/24629/chapter-18-dr-farrah-gray; see also "Dr. Farrah Gray," Speaking.com, accessed March 30, 2021, https://speaking.com/speakers/dr-farrah-gray/.
2. "Psalm 72:18," Treasury of David, Bible Study Tools, accessed March 30, 2021, https://www.biblestudytools.com/commentaries/treasury-of-david/psalms-72-18.html.

CONNECT WITH US

Connect with Bill Winston Ministries on social media. Visit www.billwinston.org/social to connect with all of his official social media channels.

Bill Winston Ministries
PO Box 947
Oak Park, Illinois 60303-0947
(708) 697-5100
(800) 711-9327
www.billwinston.org

Bill Winston Ministries Africa
22 Salisbury Road
Morningside, Durban, KWA Zulu Natal 4001
+27(0)313032541
orders@billwinston.org.za
www.billwinston.org.za

Bill Winston Ministries Canada
PO Box 2900
Vancouver, BC V6B 0L4
(844) 298-2900
www.billwinston.ca

Prayer Call Center
(877) 543-9443

More Books by Bill Winston